Horses!

It was the first day of my first summer camp at Timberline. I had gone through the check-in process, met my counselor, said a slightly nervous, but cheerful 'good bye' to my parents, sisters and brother and carried my sleeping bag and suitcase to my cabin. At that time, the cabins were away up in the ring of trees, a good five minute walk from the bunkhouse and kitchen complex through the horse pasture. I had come to camp with a school friend, also a horse nut, so our priorities aligned well. The second we plunked down our gear on a bunk bed in our cabin, we headed out on a search to find the horses.

Rockette's Story

"More beans, please!"

When we first started TR, Peter and I had no idea what camp even was—your kids know what camp is all about, they've gone to camp—but we hadn't! I had no idea, and here I was set to cook for camp. I had no idea of quantities for shopping. A 5 lb bag of corn starch was a huge amount to me! I remember one time early on, getting a camp lunch of beans, opening up a giant can of beans and setting this out. I thought this was lots! It wasn't. I opened another giant can. That was gone! I'll never forget the look on this boy's face who kept coming back, "More beans, please!"

Books by Faith Richardson

Toby's Timberline
The Orbits of Clytie Series:
☪ *Dark is a Color*
☪ *Hoverlight*
☪ *Meet the Dawn*
Angel Walker
Tree Root and River Rat
The Peacock's Stone

Toby's Timberline

by

Faith Richardson

with ***Rockette's Story:***
The History of Timberline Ranch

by **Doris Wittenberg** and **Tim Wittenberg**

as told to **Faith Richardson**

Published by Fox Song Books
Ferndale, Washington, USA

Published by Fox Song Books
PO Box 548, Ferndale WA 98248
fox@foxsongbooks.com

ISBN: 978-0-9744989-8-0   (trade paper)
Library of Congress Control Number: 2011930095

Printed in the United States of America
10 9 8 7 6 5 4 3 2 1

Dedication

For Rocky and Swede,
two men of God in word and deed.

In memory of Tim (Candy), a faithful friend.

This is written with grateful thanksgiving for the many,
many people involved in the ministry of
Timberline Ranch,
especially Rockette and Swedie,
mentors who lived out leadership
from the heart, mind, and soul.

In heartfelt appreciation of all my TR buddies—
steadfast pals through thousands of mosquito bites,
multiple rainy camp weeks,
more than a few bee stings,
and one double-barreled outhouse:
'the rancher's life was the life for us at the
ranch called Timberline!'

With special thanks to:
Topsy and Blackjack
Princess
Twilight, Melawanna, and Sunweila
Revard
Sunny
and Burrita, too

Upper left: Rocky & Rockette (Peter and Doris Wittenberg)
Above: Rocky and Swede
Left: Swede and Candy (Tim Wittenberg)
Below: Swede & Swedie (Ted and Marge Hall) leading campfire; Rocky in foreground.

Contents

May we suggest that you mail your registration
form early, as many were turned away last year.
Mail to:
Timberline Ranch
N. 224th St. RR 2
Maple Ridge, B.C.
V2X 7E7
SEE YA
THIS SUMMER
PARDNER!
Your Hosts
Mr. & Mrs.
Peter Wittenberg.
"Rocky and Rockette"

Toby's Timberline

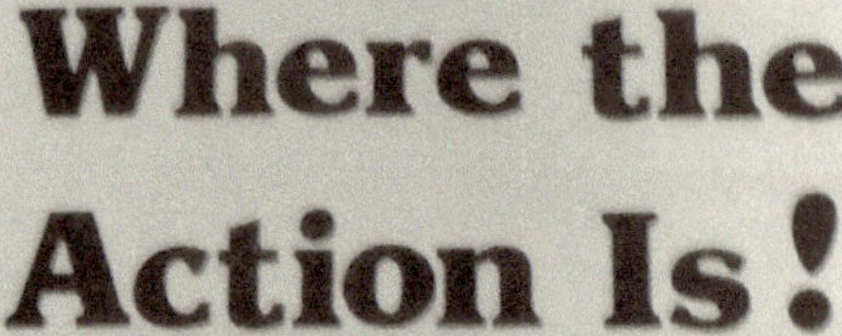

TIMBERLINE RANCH
R.R. 2, Maple Ridge, B.C.

THIS IS TO CERTIFY THAT

is a member in good standing of
the TIMBERLINE LADIES AUXILIARY.

This membership is for the year
1974 - 5

President   Sec.-Treasurer

Above:
my mom's Timberline
Ranch Ladies Auxiliary
Card, 1974-5
Below: Hard to see, but I
am 5th in the line up, on
Revard.

Preface

It seems that most book prefaces always start with the author moaning about how they were dragged into writing the book they are introducing. You will not find this here! I cheerfully proclaim that I thoroughly enjoyed every bit of this project and that no one could have wanted to do it more! I only wish it weren't finished ... I loved my reflective visits back home to Timberline as a camper and summer camp staff member.

Toby's Timberline did not start out as 'Toby's' at all. Originally, this was to have been a more serious work of history. I was quickly to learn, though, that the journey of ministry development is, like the Timberline experience itself, laced with humor and rawness of life that reveals itself best when unwrapped in the stories of encounter.

Rockette provided stories of relationships and divine meet-ups that provided a living history of Timberline Ranch—what a mentor she was to me even in this. Candy (Tim Wittenberg), who worked with the first herd of horses at the ranch, captured memories of many of those oh-so-loved equine characters. What was I to do but stand back and enjoy? They inspired me to draw on my own Timberline memories and stories of encounter. **Toby's Timberline** slowly came into being.

Writing **Toby's Timberline** became a journey 'back home' to TR. What a joy to reflect and spend time again with many of the 'Timberline pillars' with whom so many of us were privileged to be mentored. I am thankful for these men and women of God who gave of themselves so steadfastly. In hindsight, their longsuffering kindness astounds me! At Timberline, I encountered Christ lived out in faithfulness without retreat from the complexities of reality and without falling into the snare of hair-splitting dogma; I saw authentic Christian living.

This steadfast living was not only demonstrated by the 'Timberline pillars,' but by many of my staff peers. I'm immediately brought to mind of Jinx and her unfailing generous spirit, as well as the kindness of Woody in befriending me and walking alongside when I was a junior counselor.

A memory that I believe Christ brought back to me during my personal journey of faith from evangelical fundamentalism into the sacramental tradition of faith in the Catholic Church, was Rocky's calm approach to denominations and church allegiances. During one camp, as new counselors, we had created a small tempest trying to ensure that all evangelical T's were crossed and I's were dotted. I think at the time we were quite bothered because a camper had a 'catholic bible' with the deutero-canon. Rocky simply pointed us to Christ, the Redeemer. Yes, this was the word about THE Word. We didn't need to solve man-made dilemmas; we were called only to *'turn our eyes upon Jesus.'* Kind of an ironic memory for me now, but also a comforting one!

Toby's Timberline is a small reflection of the work of these men and women of God, offered in the spirit of thanksgiving for what was given to me.

I hope that ***Toby's Timberline*** will help others to journey back and remember their own Timberline Ranch experience. Echoing Rockette's words, I hope also that it provides the new generation of leadership at the ranch a knowledge of the measure of grace and miracle upon miracle of answered prayer that formed the foundation for Timberline Ranch.

There are many people to acknowledge and thank for their help and support in this project. My mom, one of the charter members of the Timberline Ranch Women's Auxiliary, not only edited drafts of the book, but is responsible for cultivating my hoarding habits. Thanks to her, I kept so much Timberline memorabilia that I had my own archives to visit—in my basement. My mom also had plenty of her own TR archives, including my letters home from camp, and many of Rocky's Timberline Ranch letters and reports. My Timberline Ranch golden horseshoe was a constant inspiration to me, as well as a few dried up circular hoof clippings from various horses ... you thought I was kidding about the 'hoarding' habit, didn't you!

I also have my many mentors at Timberline Ranch to thank. In particular I want to thank Rockette, Swede and Swedie, Curly and Curlette, Rusty and Sunny, Jinx, Candy, Nik and Chips for being on board with me so early on when this project was simply an idea. The time you spent meeting with me, allowing me to tape interviews, sending me tapes of recollections, and enjoying with me that amazing campfire back in 1995 at the ranch provided priceless stories and inspiring memories. I thank God that Swede and Candy were able to be a part of this project early on. Rocky, already in heaven when we all met up that summer, I'm sure was helping to orchestrate things from his position in the 'New Timberline' above.

Perhaps he had already placed that sign in Heaven that he had spoken about so long ago in chapel: TIMBERLINE RANCH CAMPERS THIS WAY!

I want to thank Kermit, Anita Wittenberg Tow, Rocky and Rockette's daughter and my dear friend and TR comrade for her support and the photos of our lovely Rocky and Rockette that she provided to me so quickly in response to my panicked Facebook message to her.

Thinking of additional panicked Facebook messages, so many thanks go to Levi, Holly Hall Johnson, and Ted 'Huck' Hall for providing me with pictures of their parents, our beloved Swede and Swedie, and for double checking Swede's lyrics and lyric arrangement of traditional camp songs that became TR specials.

Now that I'm on a Facebook train of thought, thanks to the TR Staff Alumnae page for the ability to post quick questions—and thanks to all those TR folk who responded, especially Odz, Little Hoss, Chips and Nik.

Craig Douglas, the current Executive Director of Timberline Ranch, deserves thanks for quickly responding to a semi-panicked email and phone message asking for permission to use early Timberline brochures and promotional materials for graphics and illustrative inspiration.

My husband, Vincent Richardson, drew very heavily on the feel of the early Timberline artwork to design the cover graphics, and by use of digital photography, he was able to drop several of these early pieces into the book to lend the feel of a scrapbook to **Toby's Timberline**. Thank you, Vincent, for all your hard work! Thanks also for letting me play Swede and Swedie's albums over and over and over again …

In the words of an early TR brochure, "Howdy, Partner! and may I add, "Welcome to **Toby's Timberline!**"

"We are Cabin Number 5"

The Timberline Theme Song
(by Ted 'Swede' Hall)

We are the campers of Timberline
We like it here where the camping's fine
We ride, we shoot with gun and bow
It's a rancher's life that we love so

Timberline, Timberline,
The rancher's life is fine! (yes, sir!)
The rancher's life is the life for me
At the ranch called Timberline.

We are the campers of Timberline
We like it here where the camping's fine
We read of Jesus in God's Word
It's the sweetest story ever heard.

I asked Swede and Swedie for the story behind the writing of the TR theme song. Because it is such an iconic Timberline memory, I was expecting quite the story. However, Swede couldn't remember any details of writing the song—just that it had been written his first or second year at Timberline (1967 or 1968), and that he wrote it while driving from TR to Seattle and back again. Swede said that he felt strongly the need for Timberline to have a theme song, so when no one else wrote one, he did. Just like Swede to see a need and quietly get it met—and met superbly!

1

The rancher's life is the life for me ...

t Timberline, we became cowboys. Male or female, small or tall, fat or thin, the rancher's life was the life for us, at the ranch called Timberline. One of my favorite memories of Timberline was on a Saturday late afternoon, four of us staff, jumping on our horses and riding to the little country store for a freezie. How perfect that the Haney corner store had a horse rail instead of a parking lot! We lived in cowboy boots and jeans, and rarely were seen without a cowboy hat. Regardless of whether we worked in the kitchen for the week, wrangled at the barn, or were camp counselors, we were first and foremost, ranchers.

Where did this ranch obsession come from? I suppose that for most of us it started with an early and unmitigated love affair with horses. For many of us, a connection between 'horse' and 'cowboy' became fused, too. Perhaps in my case, the Cowboy Peewee tee shirt I wore as a three year old was to blame for that. All I know is that recorded by a Brownie box

17

camera, there I am at three, four, seven years decked out in a cowboy outfit complete with holster and hat. Although Cowboy Peewee has long gone to tee shirt heaven, I still have the holster in a box in our basement, as well as the stick horse that took me down many a trail in our backyard. For me, 'cowboy' was a slight misnomer; 'horse girl' was a better name. Cows, although interesting in their own way, were simply a backdrop to living a life surrounded by horses. In a neighborhood game of cowboys and Indians, I moved happily back and forth; sometimes I was an Indian, sometimes I was a cowboy, and most often, I was a horse!

Can you imagine then, my exuberant joy when I heard there was a place called Timberline Ranch? My dad, a junior high school teacher, sponsored the Christian youth chapter of Interschool Christian Fellowship (ISCF) at his school. He discovered Timberline Ranch while seeking out a camp where the ISCF kids could go for a retreat. We got to visit Timberline Ranch to arrange for the retreat and I remember roaming around gazing through the wire into the big pasture drinking in the view of those horses and ponies. Every tail swish, every skin-shivering movement, hearing the crunch of hay between their teeth. What a wonderful visit. A few weeks later, we towed our house trailer out to Haney, BC, and the whole family got to attend our first weekend at Timberline Ranch.

I was nine years old. I had never seen a whole herd of horses up close. They stood side by side in the corral. Etched in my mind are these pictures: a row of saddles in a small, dusty tack room, a black pony foal kicking and bucking in a circle around his thickly-maned mother, the criss-cross marks of hooves cutting through the sod, and a line of horses crossing the bridge over a stream lined with fern and skunk cabbage. Although the camp had few amenities in the late 1960's when our family first became acquainted with it,

Timberline Ranch quickly became my metaphor for heaven. My memory of Timberline Ranch in those early years is fragrant with the good rich earth, crushed blackberry vines, and sun-baked house-sized boulders covered in moss and lichen. I hear the water squelching under the horse's feet near the swamp; smell the wood shavings underfoot and the meadow hay spilling out of the pasture rack. I remember seeing the flash of a small, light brown salamander in the pasture stream.

Over the next couple of years, Timberline Ranch became a part of our family history, as the family joined Dad's ISCF groups for weekend retreats at the ranch. I still have a copy of one of the brochures that my older sister drafted for an ISCF Christmas retreat weekend at Timberline. It was 1972 and the weekend cost was $10 per student. For $10, students got to go horseback riding, do riflery and archery, hiking and games, food and lodging—including a banquet on Saturday night with a singing group. In addition, evangelist Reverend Peter Wittenberg was scheduled as the speaker to give 'talks on Christian living.' Talk about a full weekend and an incredible bargain—even in 1972. What is funny, is that the brochure I have in my scrapbook has the registration form carefully filled out by me—including a neatly drafted forged signature of my mother in the parental permission box. I guess I really was not going to take a chance at missing out on that weekend!

There was little danger of missing that, or other weekends and events at Timberline. My parents by this time had a deep appreciation for Reverend Wittenberg, whom we quickly came to know as 'Rocky,' and recognized the value of our time at Timberline not only as social development and good, clean fun, but also of spiritual growth and soul-deep mentoring. What Timberline lacked in facilities during those years, it made up for in spades with, as one long-time camp program director, Curly, said, "Love. Timberline was all about love—the kind of love that wasn't afraid to set boundaries for kids and hold them accountable to their own God-given worth."

Speaking with Jinx, Candy, Chips, Nik, and Rockette one afternoon, a number of years ago, we mused about the lack of amenities in those early years. Our conclusion was that somehow, for us it was a good thing to have less. Although we were a smaller group back then, we had comparatively less and had to share more. Jinx pointed out, "Even outhouses! Remember, the 'Girls' outhouse had two 'holes' … and it was a good thing! Three cabins, one outhouse, you could have been out there all night waiting in line!"

Of course Jinx's statement brought up the memory of what was not so good about outhouses—the number of flashlights that rolled down and disappeared into the depths. I recall a few occasions when that outhouse had an eerie glow coming from it very early in the morning. I also recall, the very helpful Jinx being lowered down to retrieve one with a coat hanger. Yes, Timberline staffers are a resilient, innovative, and hardy group, always ready to provide assistance where needed—but, Jinx, that was definitely going above and beyond the call of duty!

Many TR staff have done just that: taken to heart the call to serve. Curly, like many of those early staff members, annually devoted time to Timberline camps, relocating his wife (Curlette) and their growing family from their home a province away to come to Timberline for a few weeks every summer. Rusty and Sunny were another couple who volunteered time and energy, traveling from their homes in the United States to come to this small town of Haney, BC, and give of themselves to mentor young camp counselors and nurture campers in Timberline's rich environment of boundless love for God, the creation, and kids.

Swede and Swedie, also from the United States, gave entire summers and sabbatical times to the ministry of Timberline Ranch, leading music, becoming puppeteers and master story tellers, and experts at reading heart-deep needs of campers and young staff alike. At one point they relocated their family for two years to live at the Ranch. In the very first edition of the **Timberline Times** (1974), Rocky wrote under **News Bits**:

> *"'Swede & Swedie' have driven 500 miles (one way) to be with us for our four week-end camps—they sure must love you campers eh?! Swede has some terrific new magic tricks—they sure keep ya guessing ????????"*

What was it that drew these people from their professions and daily lives to come to Timberline Ranch—at that time, a place of mud, mosquitos, perpetual building projects, floods, and shared bathrooms? I know what brought kids out to Timberline; at least initially, it was the horses and living on a real, honest-to-goodness ranch. Horses brought kids out, but the staff kept them there, and kept them coming back. Why would a law professor, teachers, business people, known musicians, and other professionals return again and again to give of themselves?

At that time Timberline was roughly made up of horse pasture, swamp, and very few, well-used buildings. The early Timberline brochures refer to rustic cabins, and indeed they were rustic! As an 11-year-old, I remember being thrilled that our cabin in the trees was 'on stilts' and that I could reach through the floorboards and pat Topsy and Blackjack, who sheltered there for protection from the rain. There was a washhouse and one running tap up in the circle of cabins, and there were outhouses. Yes, indeed, the girls' outhouse was a two-seater. We thought this was a great invention, given the 'scariness' of leaving the sanctuary of your cabin at night. Girls always went in groups!

The main camp had a bunkhouse/dining room and kitchen complex with one Mens' and one Womens' bathroom behind it. The dining room was the largest room with the kitchen attached on the far end. I do recall being so pleased as a kid to sit in the dining room with horse pictures on the walls and notice that small bits of straw protruded from a few of the half-rounds that lined the inside and outside of the bunkhouse. We guessed that the bunkhouse had been insulated with straw and felt this was so very 'old west.' I don't know if it really was or not, but that was my camper-cowboy fantasy. I also loved the fact that we had to walk across a real cattle grid to get back and forth from our cabins back to the main camp. I remember stepping with pride in my scuffed cowboy boots (the more battered your boots were, the better) across the cattle grid rails, thinking that I really was living the cowboy's life.

At one end of the horse pasture, bordering the swamp, stood a tiny tack shop/hay barn that was home base for a small herd of horses and ponies who, although fiercely loved by campers, for the most part, would have looked out of place in a show ring. Down towards the road, also bordering the swamp that formed a semi-circle around the property stood two small houses. One of these houses was home to Rocky, the camp director, and his family. The other smaller house was lodging for the volunteer staff families, usually the program directors for a series of camps. It was also, in those early years, the first aid station. Swede and Swedie recall staying in that little house along with many uninvited critters! Talk about the cowboy life! That house was very old and was taken down in the years following to make room for a newer, bigger, 'house on the rock.' But, at that time, these few, very rustic buildings were the measure of Timberline Ranch. Somehow, Timberline was immensely more than the sum of its parts.

The ranchers life is the life for me ...

The bunkhouse, at the time of this writing, remains at Timberline today, but in the early days, along with the kitchen and dining room, as I recall, there were a couple of areas for sleeping and a storage area. One room doubled as a sleeping room when needed, or a lounge and meeting area, where counselors and staff got together, and prayer meetings and devotions were held. I recall chapel being held there too, although fairly rapidly camps overflowed the small room and spilled out onto the boardwalk. This room eventually became Candy's Cave, the Tuck shop. The bunkhouse was, and is, noted for its long boardwalk with an overhang, and big wooden steps leading up and down from both ends. A hitching post and horse rail ran the length of the boardwalk. We loved the western feel of the bunkhouse and we adored that boardwalk. Our boots sounded so good on it!

With every new camp the boardwalk became the hangout site for campers and counselors almost immediately. The cabins, earlier on, were located up through the horse pasture in the trees, the dining room was off limits except for mealtimes, and Candy's Cave didn't exist yet. The boardwalk was the spot to be. I recall listening to the music of Swede and Swedie, or other country-style gospel singing coming through the speakers as we sat in groups on the railings and laughed and chatted on that boardwalk. This was the site for mosquito bite counting contests, and the telling of the tales of the morning: did you get to ride your favorite horse? Did your group get to gallop? Who shot a bulls-eye? What did you do for Cabin Clean up?

The boardwalk also was the place for announcements and prayer just before meals. Campers would line up in straight lines perpendicular to the boardwalk (if it wasn't raining!) or up and down the boardwalk if it was raining. The straighter the line, the quicker Swedie's eagle eyes would spot your good behavior and allow your cabin into the dining room.

Those boardwalk steps were filled with anticipation, fun and laughter, but they were also the site of deep conversations. The boardwalk steps were a great place for, as Curly said to me, 'time outs and heart-to-hearts.' Curly was most often the program director for Junior Boys' camps. He recalls talking with a boy who had been fighting, and this young man finding Christ right there on the bunkhouse steps. For many searching kids, the door to Heaven was an easy reach from Timberline soil—and those bunkhouse boardwalk steps.

Junior Boys camps could be challenging for the director and staff because of little-boy energy and aggression. But there were many troubled kids of all ages and both genders. The ranchers' life attracted so many who were seeking a different life from what they knew. At that time, Timberline had a high percentage of children and teens attending camps that were, what was dubbed at the time 'Ministry' kids, meaning they were in the care of government agencies rather than living with parents. Most often these children were no different in behavior or attitude than any of the other children and teens attending camp; sometimes, however, they had challenges and came across as 'tough' kids. These kids were used to being overlooked and had a hardened attitude from needing to look out for themselves. Within a couple of days, most found the 'Timberline difference.'

The Timberline difference in dealing with 'tough' kids was the TR staff themselves. They genuinely were rooting for these kids. There was hopeful expectation that they would turn around and joy when each one would respond more and more with each passing day. There was only heartbreak and a sense of failure among the staff when, rarely, a camper had to be sent home.

Swedie recalls that every once in a while Rocky would have to make a decision to send a kid home:

The ranchers life is the life for me ...

It was always a heartbreak and we tried every way of getting through to these kids before the decision had to be made; usually because there had been some physical threat of violence, or fight. But, in those rare cases where a kid had to be sent home, there seemed to be a sense of relief in the camp and the whole atmosphere of the week improved—so I suppose that was an affirmation that it needed to be. That said, there was always a sense that we failed when someone had to be sent home. You know, everyone was rooting for the tough, troubled kids. And so often Monday and Tuesday might be very difficult in the week of camp, but by Wednesday, things would turn around, hearts would soften, kids would open up and be less guarded. The camp would become cohesive and by Friday, no one was looking forward to going home the next day. Wednesdays were days filled with small, but very real miracles!

Rusty and Sunny most often were program directors for mixed teens and younger mixed camps. Behaviours that were challenging in Junior Boys and Girls camps often are even more concerning in teens, as they are much bigger and more able to act on aggressive feelings and long standing habits. Sunny recounted to me how Rusty and Rocky were doing a routine walk through of a teens camp and happened on a group of boys beginning a chain fight. I asked Rusty how he and Rocky had stopped such violent behavior. Rusty paused and thought about it a minute. Sunny smiled and said that Rocky simply told them that fighting just was not done here. Rather amazingly, the chains were handed over and there was no more trouble from these teens for the remainder of camp. Rusty and Sunny continued the story, saying, "campers knew, in a deep way, that we were all 'on board' for these kids—from the staff in the kitchen to the wranglers in the barn to the counselors and camp director— we were here seeking to be Christ to these kids and they saw it."

Curly and Curlette agreed, adding that campers and young staff, too, saw love that wasn't afraid to be lived out, "Love that included the discipline needed to keep everyone safe and happy. Many of these troubled kids who were kept in line left at the end of the week changed and just wept when they had to go home."

The early years at Timberline saw too, a mix of staff that ranged from openly Christian individuals, to youth from Christian families, and from frankly troubled kids with little to no church upbringing of any kind. I recall one summer there were a number of older adolescents, under care of the Ministry, living at the Ranch and involved in working on the grounds and building projects. These youth were expected to live in accord with Timberline standards, and for the most part, they did. There were many deep and heartfelt conversations around the campfire or dining room table after the campers had left for home. Rocky expected the ranch to truly come together in daily chapel and that included ALL staff! Surprisingly, these youth, although they grumbled at times and kept up a veneer of toughness, truly appreciated Rocky and Swede and other weekly camp leaders. I remember Odz, Nik, Jinx and I smiling when we would see 'tough' staff begin to melt under the Timberline atmosphere.

In one of Rocky's annual reports (1972) he makes mention of this program:

> *"A 'preventive care' for 'Teen boys is still a great possibility for Timberline—staff and proper facilities are holding us back. For the past two years we have had two or three boys nearly all the time but this entails much extra work. A young boy, who was not wanted by his parents, stayed with us for a time, but because of the above reasons we felt we could not keep him and he was placed in another home. To-day he is in prison. We feel badly, for had he been able to stay at*

the Ranch he may have been following the Lord and learning to be a useful citizen. Continue to pray with us re: this open door of service to help disadvantaged boys."

When I first went to Timberline as a camper and then as a counselor, all the Timberline camps were two weeks long. At the time, there were no hot showers for campers so there was pressure from health and safety to either provide bathing facilities or shorten camps. At the same time, there was a growing demand for more camps; potential campers were being placed on waiting lists. The decision was made by Rocky and the Timberline board to move from two week to one week camps. We, 'two week' veterans mourned the loss of two week camps. As campers, of course, we did not see the need for hot showers—after all we went swimming in the river all the time, but I'm sure others thought differently! Swede and Swedie, however, and many of the program directors, had a different concern. They wondered if the change from two week to one week camps would change the dynamics of camp, the 'Timberline difference,' especially for the 'tough' kids that needed time to melt into Timberline life. Swedie recalls asking, "How can we make a difference in a kid's life in only one week?" Swedie answered her own question for me, "We were afraid, but we were wrong. The change just happened quicker!"

The Timberline difference; love for Christ, creation and others, lived out regardless of amenities. There was an energy of care and a blanket of prayer that covered the campers, the staff, the horses, and, yes, even that bunkhouse boardwalk.

Second verse. Same as the first. A little bit louder and a little bit worse!

Third verse same as the first a little bit louder and a whole lot worse!

Fourth verse. Same as the first. A whole lot louder and a whole lot worse!

The horse went around with his foot on the ground. The horse went around with his foot on the ground the horse went around with his foot on the ground the horse went around with his foot on the ground

The horse went around!

2

Horses!

It was the first day of my first summer camp at Timberline. I had gone through the check-in process, met my counselor, said a slightly nervous, but cheerful 'good bye' to my parents, sisters and brother and carried my sleeping bag and suitcase to my cabin. At that time, the cabins were away up in the ring of trees, a good five minute walk from the bunkhouse and kitchen complex through the horse pasture. I had come to camp with a school friend, also a horse nut, so our priorities aligned well. The second we plunked down our gear on a bunk bed in our cabin, we headed out on a search to find the horses.

We weren't alone. Most of the campers had the same idea. The horses were grazing in a loose herd and campers dotted the pasture, trailing horses and trying to sneak in a few pats here and there as the kind, but wary horses moved in one direction or another. We quickly joined up with the unofficial Timberline tour director, who we would come to know as Candy. Candy introduced us, one horse at a time, to Timberline's herd. We learned about Blackjack and Adarin, the Welsh ponies who doubled as escape artists, Topsy, the retired gymkhana star, Princess and her sensitive ears, Marylegs, the tallest horse in TR history and possibly the world, her faithful companion and ex race horse, Ben, Rocky's lead horse, Patches, with one blue eye, the moody Dusky, pale delicate Shadow, who birthed the wary Fresca, and, finally, Shawney who always wore a hat for special occasions and who, according to Candy, had been in foal for several years (at least that is how I understood it!).

Up till now, Topsy had always been my girl—the very first horse, well, pony—I had ridden on my own that first weekend we had, as a family, been a part of my Dad's ISCF group retreat at Timberline. Topsy was also the mother of my own pony, Twilight. Though I didn't know it at that moment, Topsy was about to be dethroned in my heart. Not because she had changed, but because the friend that I had come with fell head over heels for Topsy and would NOT ride anyone else. She was in my riding group. I was heartbroken. That is, until I rode Princess and fell in love all over again! Just now, though, here I stood on that sunny Sunday afternoon, surrounded by horses, including the beloved Topsy, and two whole weeks of horse heaven stretched out in front of me.

That first TR camp that I attended, I was not just a camper; I was there to 'help out' at the barn. I realize now that this was a kindly way of allowing me to be at camp—on a scholarship of sorts. My parents could not have afforded the full cost of camp; ranch director Rocky created a work opportunity for me to attend Junior Girls camp. I could not have been happier, and I took my job very seriously—probably much more so than Rocky could have imagined. I would spend every spare minute at the barn helping out by carrying hay, fetching tack, leading horses, scooping poop.

Horses!

The TR wranglers were my heroes; I think I was too shy to get into much of a conversation with them, but they were kind to this tagalong horse-crazy girl. I soaked up every minute at the barn, learning the details of each Timberline horse, carrying saddles and bridles to the designated spots under the horses' name tags. I even learned how to bridle Princess who had an ear phobia. I remember watching the wranglers swing into the saddle with such assurance. I met the legend known as Laredo, a weight lifter. They said he could lift a horse, and, later I was to find out this was true! He would become known for carrying Miss Wonder around, as a foal. Of course, I remember Hoss's good natured laugh that could be heard from one end of the ranch to the other! I also remember Poncho, the only girl wrangler at the time. She had cracked the 'hay loft' ceiling, so to speak, of this male-dominated corral, so was quite admired by all horse-crazy girls.

When does the untreatable condition of 'horse crazy' begin? I wish I could recall the moment I saw my first horse, for I think it began then. Did I, through the glass of our family Ford, see a colt full of youthful joy galloping through a meadow dotted with dandelions? Or did a kindly graying muzzle reach out in curiosity at this baby in a stroller out for a visit? Maybe a rotund shaggy pony trotted through the spread of a children's book that my mother read to my sister and me? I'll never know, but in those seconds when eyes connected with equine, something happened to rewire my developing brain from neophyte to horse lover. To this day, endorphins explode with the nicker, swiveling ear, or soft muzzle of a horse.

I do remember very faintly the first horse I was lifted onto: a white broad back with a scanty mane running down a giraffe-long neck that stretched down into the green grass; I sat on a veritable horse-mountain. The second experience is more locked into my brain. I got to ride on a beautiful bay mare with a long striding walk, obediently led by the son of a friend of my parents. Around and around the paddock we went, every hoof beat etched in the core of my horse-loving soul. This time I sat on a real English saddle—creaking, aromatic leather and all. The third horse event for me was meeting our new neighbor's horse, Joe. Joe was a patient, dark bay gelding who allowed his teenage owner to ride him without a bit. Joe smelled heavenly to me and I picked handfuls of clover just to be near him. He would very amiably stroll over and lower a friendly head over the fence to accept my tasty bouquets whenever he happened to notice me. But it was Timberline's Topsy who holds top billing in my memory for being the first pony I rode without a lead line.

Nothing about Topsy was modern: from her thick sticking-out mane to her round belly and dull, well-worn saddle. But Topsy shone. Topsy was kind and sensible with a modicum more common sense than most of us campers had at the time. Topsy was an honest mare who did her job well; she taught me and innumerable campers how to ride. Topsy was special to me in another way, too. Topsy was the mother of Twilight, my first pony. It was Twilight who was the young foal that I had seen gamboling about the horse pasture on my very first visit to Timberline. I didn't know at the time that my parents would end up buying Twilight as a weanling for me.

It is not that I hadn't been campaigning for a gift of this exact nature; every Christmas and birthday the first thing on my wish list was HORSE OR PONY. The earliest family story of my horse-crazy nature tells the tale of me answering my dad's breakfast-table question of, 'so, how did you sleep?' with, 'like a horse!' ... demonstrating by putting both arms together and legs together and lying on my side. I longed to know horses from the inside out.

Horses!

With Twilight, I got my desire with a vengeance! My parents were far from being horse people. In hindsight, I think they thought that giving me a pony colt was like giving me a puppy—we would grow up together. With any normal child, giving them a half-grown stud colt would have turned them forever off anything horse. For me, it forced me past the Disney-like dream of horse-human paranormal connection and made me dig deeper into learning how to take care of and train this ball of pony energy.

My scrapbook at that time is full of brochures and horse equipment catalogs, articles clipped from the Western Horseman on horse training, and diagrams of horses' hooves and overall anatomy. I remember my joy when I found an old copy of the British Pony Club manual in a library book sale. I practically memorized it. My parents had bought me a small paperback book from the feed store called, *Ponies as Pets*, by Robert Gannon. It is in pieces, but I still have it. I felt as though I knew each one of the kids photographed with their ponies throughout that little book. As I grew older, the two books I checked out of our school library most frequently were, *Heads Up—Heels Down*, by C.W. Anderson, and the unlikely, *Common Sense Horsemanship*, by Vladimir S. Littauer, a former Captain in the Russian Imperial Cavalry, which was far above my grasp. I could quote passages from both of them, but especially from *Heads Up—Heels Down*. C.W. Anderson was a wonderful rider and illustrator of all things horse and knew how to teach the most ignorant horse lover—me!

Twilight was a character and a half who, even after he was gelded, became the leader of whatever herd he found himself in. He led great escapes over stall doors and under fences and had a wonderful time corrupting other horses and leading them into dicey situations. Twilight was smart and learned quickly, and he somehow chose to put up with me in the process. Everyone, except my neighbors with the immaculate garden which Twilight chose to visit in daring night raids, liked this perky, black Welsh pony with the star, stripe, and snip on his nose. Twilight came to Timberline with me for several summers of camp, working the line with his mother, Topsy, and half-sister Melawanna, who my parents had also purchased for my sister. Poor Mel, a patient, gentle filly by Blackjack out of Princess, was often led astray by her mischievous half-brother, although she enjoyed the neighbor's garden perhaps even more than Twilight!

My favorite memories of Twilight at Timberline are of racing through flooded sections of the gravel road in the early dawn. Rusty and his owner, Nik on Princess, and other staff from time to time would join us. It was always a special moment to join up with Rocky on Patches or Pepper out for an early morning ride, too. It was a heartbreak when my legs began to grow longer than Twilight's and, as a teen, I grew self-conscious about riding a pony. I graduated to another horse at Timberline, Revard, but Twilight remained the number one boy in my heart for many years. Several years later, my palomino gelding, Sunny, spent some time at Timberline Ranch, working the line too, while I was attending university. It felt good to be a part of Timberline even in this more distant way.

We all have favorite memories of Timberline horses, some special moments of connection and learning, others sheer fun and filled with the craziness of unique characters and odd situations. As wranglers, hanging out at the barn, we had many lively moments with the horses and ponies. One moment for me was a result of boasting about how fast Twilight was able to get up to top speed. Of course, that sparked a series of short 'drag' races across the end of the corral. I was right—Twilight beat the pants off the other ponies—but he did it by himself. I remember the "ready, set,

GO," and then, all of a sudden there I was flat on my back staring up into the blue sky. Twilight had literally run out from under me!

Nik had a special connection to Princess, the pinto with the amazing floating canter and the ear phobia. Princess had become my favourite when, at my first TR camp, my friend had wrestled Topsy away from me. We were lucky enough to board Princess for one winter at our home in Richmond, BC. We owned two of Princess's foals: Melawanna and Sunweila. Sunweila was born one spring morning at dawn in our pasture, the year we boarded Princess. But there was no denying the bond between Nik and Princess, who became a team for many years. Besides, Twilight had already taken the top spot in my heart by then! I believe that Princess thrived under the 'ownership' of Nik. Princess was a smart mare who taught all her riders to have light hands—she would gently manage to pull the reins, little by little, until she had full mouth freedom! Some years later, Nik was instrumental in arranging to have Princess bred. She became the happy owner of her foal, which she named Princess Tara.

One of Nik and Chips favourite stories about the horses was the tale of 747, the biggest horse on the ranch (post Merrylegs). Nik describes him was a giant palomino with a small brain. Where the TR petting zoo is now, there used to be nothing but swamp—deep muck and bush, beaver, and skunk cabbage. At the time of 747, workers had just dug a deep ditch to try to drain an area of the swamp, but the ramps hadn't been put in yet to access the new bridge to cross the new ditch. Nik tells the tale:

One morning, the wranglers were feeding the horses, and they came to me and said, "747's missing." Well, he wasn't in the field, so I got in my car and drove around to both neighbors, but no one had seen him, and I couldn't find any sign of him. Then I wondered if he had got into the creek. So I said to the wranglers, "I'll go get some straps, just in case we need to pull him out of the creek." I had just started down to the barn, when not twenty feet away—just off the new bridge that had no ramps up to it yet—in an old creek bed in the swamp, I saw a head and a patch of rump, that was all. 747. He was buried in mud up to his neck. We couldn't get any machinery in there, because the bridge wasn't complete. Yes, we had to pull him out by hand. It took hours. The whole camp eventually gathered there, and with every new person watching came more advice and a new miraculous idea for getting him out. We eventually dug and pulled him out. Poor 747 was in shock, so the vet was called. All was well that ended well, but you can imagine the mud. Freda was cook at that camp, and her staff was out along with everyone else mesmerized, watching 747's rescue operations. We were supposed to have pork and beans for lunch that day, and she had sent some kitchen staff to get them going. When they didn't return, Freda eventually went out looking for them, yelling, "Where are the beans??!! Where are the beans??!!" It echoed all over camp and became that summer's catchphrase: "Where are the beans?!"

Moving from the ridiculous to the sublime, Nik recalled to me a story about Applejack, who was a somewhat awkward-looking part Appaloosa gelding born on the ranch. Applejack eventually outgrew his gangly oddness and actually became the boss horse for the herd. He always led the horses into the barn, was first to enter the field with the others following; as herd leader he was always first to feed on the hay dropped in the field. One afternoon, Nik said, as she drove onto the ranch, she passed by the horses that were out in the field behind the houses. Everything looked normal; she saw Applejack and the others grazing or standing around as usual.

Horses!

Nik went out to the barn and prepared for feeding the herd, eventually opening the gates and calling in the horses. The herd soon ran in—but Applejack wasn't first. Nik thought, "That's strange," but figured he'd wander in any minute. But he didn't. So she went back out of the barn and called and called. Nothing. Concerned now, Candy and Nik then went out into the field, calling all the while. They saw Applejack up on the bank, close to the fence line. He was up on his feet, spinning in circles like he was tied. He obviously could hear them, but just wouldn't come. So Nik and Candy went closer to him.

They stopped dead in their tracks. As they got closer to Applejack, they saw Miss Wonder, one of Topsy's grown fillies. She had tried to jump the new wire fence and was hung up so that she couldn't move. Thankfully, Miss Wonder wasn't hurt—in fact, as they drew closer, it was evident that the grass truly was greener on the other side—Miss Wonder was grazing! But one wire was tight under her belly and her hind legs were suspended in the air, jammed into a second wire. Nik and Candy, being the resourceful wranglers they were, pulled out pliers, clipped the wire, and walked Miss Wonder through the fence. They let her go and she ran into the field where they had spread out the hay. Applejack followed her. Like the good leader he was, Applejack, steadfastly would not leave Miss Wonder until she had been rescued.

Talk about a lesson in loyalty and leadership! What do horses teach campers at Timberline Ranch? Rocky, Nik, Chips, Tim and others of us have over the years had discussions about the draw of horses and why they are so key to the ministry of Timberline. I'm not sure we ever came to a conclusion, or ever really could. I can tell you only my story and bits and pieces of others' stories as they have shared them with me. Toby's Timberline is filled with servants of the Lord who happen to have four legs, a mane and a tail, and immeasurable patience. I have seen rough and tough teens hugging their favorite horse with tears in their eyes; I have seen timid, insecure kids transformed by riding a humble giant like Merrylegs or 747; I have seen frantic children learn to listen to the movement of their mount's ears and twitch of a tail. I have apprehended grace and forgiveness, and I have learned about steadfast faith, obedience to duty and simple kindness from the horses of Timberline. Do horses have a part in the soul healing ministry at Timberline Ranch?

Without a doubt.

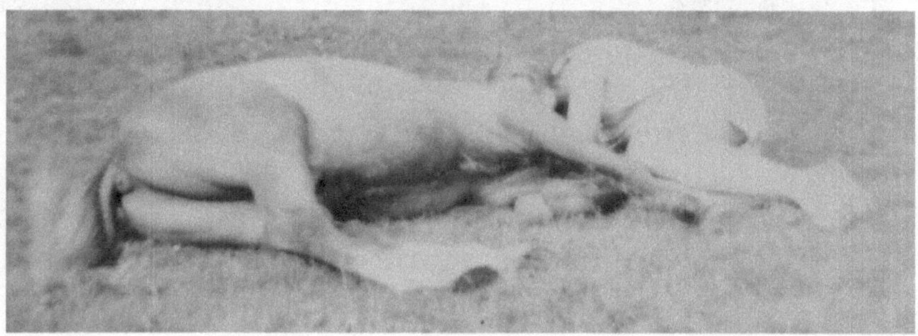

Horses!

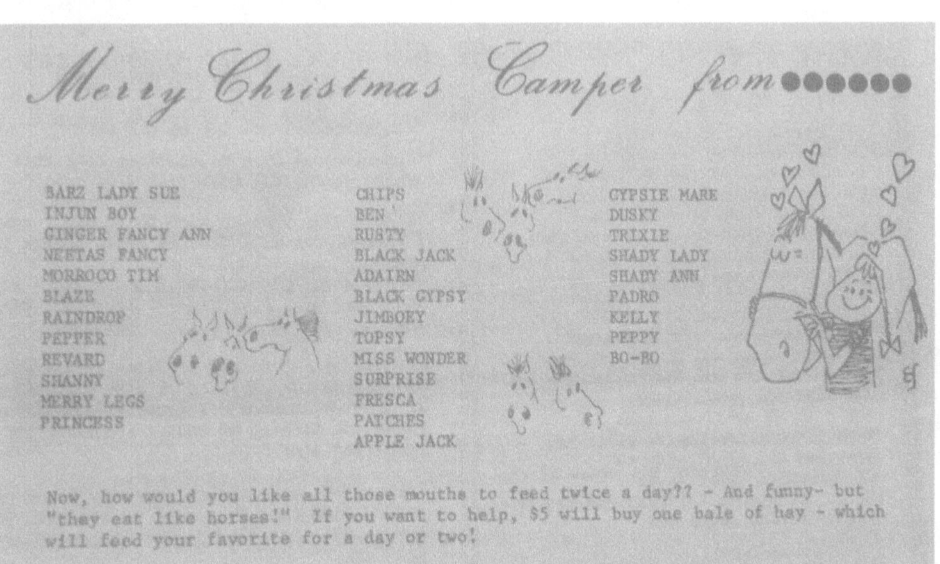

BARZ LADY SUE	CHIPS	GYPSIE MARE
INJUN BOY	BEN	DUSKY
GINGER FANCY ANN	RUSTY	TRIXIE
NEETAS FANCY	BLACK JACK	SHADY LADY
MORROCO TIM	ADAIRN	SHADY ANN
BLAZE	BLACK GYPSY	PADRO
RAINDROP	JIMBOEY	KELLY
PEPPER	TOPSY	PEPPY
REVARD	MISS WONDER	BO-BO
SHANNY	SURPRISE	
MERRY LEGS	FRESCA	
PRINCESS	PATCHES	
	APPLE JACK	

Now, how would you like all those mouths to feed twice a day?? - And funny- but "they eat like horses!" If you want to help, $5 will buy one bale of hay - which will feed your favorite for a day or two!

Many of you may not remember the Horsie, Horsie round, but in the 1970's horse-crazy Junior girls loved it!

Jinx and I remembered it during a wonderful campfire we had with Swede, Swedie, Curly, Curlette, Rusty, Sunny, Nik and Chips in August, 1995. The perfect campfire!

Horsie, Horsie (round)

Horsie, horsie, on your way
We've been together for many a day,
So let your tail go swish, your wheels go round,
Giddy up, we're homeward bound!

I like to ride my horse and buggy
As we go riding through the town
I like to hear ol' Dobbin's clip clop,
I like to see the wheels go round!

The Doodlebug Song

Poor little bug on the wall,
Ain't got no mommy at all
No one to hold him near.
No one to call him dear.

Poor little bug on the wall.
Poor little bug on the wall.

Ain't got no clothes on at all

Ain't got no hot pink shirt!
Ain't got no miniskirt!

Poor little bug on the wall.
Oooh, ooh, ooh, ooh ...

This song reminds me of Swedie. And, I must say; only Swedie and Jinx together can do this song true justice. You really have to rock the 'Ain't got no hot pink shirt! Ain't got no miniskirt!' to pull it off. Swing those hips! The rest of the song needs to be sung most tenderly, with heart-breaking pathos oozing out of your voice. Yes, one special TR memory! Swedie deserves an Oscar for her performance of 'poor little bug'!

3

Camp living and Cabin clean up

For us Junior Girl campers, Cabin Cleanup had nothing to do with picking up dirty socks and sweeping the cabin floor. Oh, that got done, all right, but it definitely wasn't the focus of our collective energy. For many cabins, it was enough to have a spotless cabin and a rock-bordered path to the door, with the word 'welcome' spelled out in buttercups. For us, this was kindergarten. No, we had elaborate plans that usually incorporated a theme and necessitated intricate scenes, like dioramas.

For example, one time we sculpted a well out of rocks and mud and created two figures out of stuffed clothes and pillow cases. One was Jesus and one was the woman at the well. We even had water in our well. We often tried to depict the scriptural story that Rocky had spoken about in Chapel the day before. That same week, we portrayed Jesus walking across the water. Thankfully, one of us had a blue sleeping bag that became our Sea of Galilee. There was Jesus, in Odz' flip flops, looking a bit rotund but with very skinny broomstick legs balanced on the sea, facing a boat made out of carefully concealed suitcases covered with a brown sleeping bag. Inside were various disciples, cheerfully attired in splashy summer girls' clothes.

We had a lot riding on our cabin cleanup plans. First, we had Swedie's daily report of the state of the cabins following supper. As Junior Girls Camp Director, Swedie was the inspector of the cabins. First of all, we wanted to impress Swedie and to hear her report of our cabin. Swedie was painstaking and highly entertaining in her reports so they were fun. But more than that, Swedie 'got' our scenes and efforts and described them as we wanted them to be seen, not like, I'm very sure in hindsight, the reality! She saw the Sea of Galilee; she saw the woman at the well, just like we had. It was worth every minute of our effort when Swedie gave her report.

The second reason we put so much effort into cabin cleanup was that along with her report, Swedie gave points. At the end of the week, if your cabin got the most points, you won the Cabin Cleanup award. Although the Cabin Cleanup award was fun, the honor of being top cabin was the real reward.

The Cabin Cleanup award was a giant shared banana split sundae— which Swede and Swedie delivered in two long 'pig troughs'. One trough was for one side of the table; the other trough was for the other side of the table. Swede really loaded those troughs. They were works of art! Digging into them as a cabin was fun, and we got to see the envious eyes of the campers that hadn't won. Swedie got into the action with a giant spoon, but I think Swede preferred his own more hygienic bowl.

Cabin groups were really the basic unit of camp life: your cabin group was your family for the week. Although as campers we were in larger groups for the day's activities, we returned to our cabins for meals and bedtime. As in a family home, there were quiet, and sometimes hilarious, conversations before breakfast and while settling down to sleep. Like any family, cabin groups went through their share of petty squabbles and longsuffering putting-up-with snorers and gigglers. I remember being amazed at the sonorous tones of a rather fastidious girl the minute she fell asleep. Her snores could be heard across to the next cabin. But somehow, we managed to sleep. It must have been the open air non-stop activity each day.

As a camper, my cabin counselor, Stripes, was like a big sister to us all, and that is what I aspired to be when I became a counselor myself. Our camp program director (for Junior Girls this was Swedie) became very much our mentor, not only in spiritual development, but in leadership. To me, and many of my peer counselors, Swedie demonstrated a way of *being* that to this day I hold as my example of authentic Christian maturity. As a counselor under Swedie, I learned to recognize when a camper needed some one-on-one attention and when a camper needed a gentle, but firm push out the door. I learned that reverent prayer has room for humor. From Swedie I also learned that our labels were meaningless when it came to the work of Christ. Swedie laid down the foundation for me to accept that in the complexity of life, there is the very simple truth of God's love.

Swede and Swedie were highly talented musicians with several albums; also they were professionals and academics with careers, and they were family people with growing children. By 'normal' standards, they should have been rushed, directive, and assigned assistants to take care of the minutiae (us!). Instead, they were simple, friendly, steadfast servant-leaders. They enjoyed laughing and chatting and sharing with each one of us as campers, as teenagers, as counselors and staff who were eager to be a part of TR ministry, but often, let me say it of myself, naïve and rather foolish at times! They had clear, but quiet boundaries around family and personal time. There was no drama about these boundaries; it was clear though, that family was family. When a new record album appeared, there was no fanfare or red carpet. I never knew until years later how extensive Swede's song writing talents were, and how well thought of Ted and Marge Hall were in the music world.

I didn't know it at the time, but what I was seeing demonstrated at Timberline in this hub of cabin living was how to be, not merely do Christian living. I was learning something at TR that I am just now recognizing: I was learning how to be authentic. I was learning how to sift out the real gold from the glitter. I was learning how to live in love.

Looking back, I see God's orchestration in sending my family—and me—to Timberline. Life as a camper, then as a counselor living the cabin life, and also living the staff life in the 'under construction' hotel meant my days were never solely my own, they were to be shared. What a wonderful lesson for a teenager to learn! Looking back I have become even more aware of the wonderful humor of God in teaching us these foundational lessons. We experienced, layered into cabin and hotel living at Timberline, moments of fright, weak-kneed laughter, tender weeping, and spirit-charged awe. We never knew in what order these would occur!

In the early years, the Timberline cabins were high in the tree line, above the horse pasture. The TR brochure called them 'rustic' and we loved every inch of these rough timbered homes on stilts with working barrel-shaped pot-belly stoves, and knotholes in the floors. We lived with nature; from the ponies that gathered below the cabin, to the bats and swallows that often shot in through the door. I can recall one season, a family of bats taking up residence in the eaves of my cabin. It actually became a comforting sound for me, hearing the family leave through the chimney pipe to go on their nighttime hunts. We all learned that it truly is folklore that bats get tangled up in your hair, but there were some eerie moments of learning this lesson. I think most of us wore a hat to bed the first couple of nights! Interestingly, I had the fewest mosquito bites that summer—thanks, I'm sure, to those bats.

Chips shared with me a story of his own as counselor in a Junior Boys camp:

I remember one camp where I was counselor in cabin one. I was heading back to the cabin after campfire and one of my campers came running up to me, saying, "Chips, Chips, there's a skunk in our cabin!" I opened the door to the cabin and cautiously looked in, but only saw one of the campers sitting on his bed. I said to the other boy, "That's not very nice--calling Allan a skunk." But then I saw movement under Allan's bunk. "Come out here," I said as calmly as possible to Allan. I called Swede, who came over, strumming his guitar, and told him of our visitor. Swede continued strumming and said, "I'll go get the tomato juice." Swede never got excited over anything!

Other than bats, the occasional squeak and scratching in the walls of a mouse, skunks and beaver in the swamp, the other most familiar, non-equine critters were frogs and snakes. Because Timberline had large areas of swamp and flood plain areas, frogs thrived. I remember driving the gravel road to and from Timberline in the evening and the road being alive with little frogs—jumping in all directions. Frog music surrounded us. The snakes thrived because the frogs thrived. There was rarely a day when you didn't see a little garter snake. I remember Huck and other Junior Boys being in Frog and Snake heaven. Their pockets would be full of them! I also very clearly remember Swedie announcing firmly to the campers lined up in front of the bunkhouse to go into the dining hall, ***"No snakes inside!"***

Living at the ranch year round meant that bigger wildlife was fairly frequently seen: deer, beaver, and the occasional black bear. I recall Kermit, Rocky's daughter and one of the 'Timberline kids,' excitedly telling me about the bear that kept her and the other TR kids stuck in the hotel for a few hours before they could run home to their families. I never saw any bears at Timberline, but I do remember one summer when we had a couple of young cougars hanging around. I most remember the wide eyes of Jinx telling us that on her morning run she had seen two cougars sunning themselves on the roof of an older, unused cabin! Later that evening, I was so sure that I saw the glint of cougar eyes in the flickering light of the campfire as I looked out into the dark stand of trees.

The Timberline kids, as we called them, had a unique perspective on the ranch. Living year round on the ranch with their parents, they experienced the seasons and ebb and flow of camp life intermingling with their own worlds of school and family. I think that I can say that most of us summer staff envied the Timberline kids. They got to stay at the end of camp. They got to come home after school to Timberline Ranch. As I grew older, though, I realized that they also had quite a sacrifice to make for this life—they had to share their parents with me and literally hundreds of other kids and teens. We appreciated their good humor in letting us into their lives, and we loved learning from them about the after-camp Timberline Ranch.

What I didn't know at the time was that the Timberline kids sometimes envied us. There is a crazy story about Huck as a young Timberline kid being quite jealous of campers and staff who got hurt and fussed over, taken to the hospital, and came back with casts or bandages or a sore arm due to a tetanus shot. Huck didn't want a cast. He'd seen his sister having to wear a full leg and arm cast for several weeks, and although she got around quite well with them (wearing the bottom completely off the foot part), it didn't look like much fun. Somehow he became fixated with the idea of going to the hospital and getting a tetanus shot. A big fussing rush to the hospital, 'sore' arm (they didn't look that bad!), lots of attention, maybe ice cream … what could be more alluring? So Huck coaxed Kermit and his sisters into his scheme. They went into the Timberline workshop where building supplies were piled up in huge stacks and began a search for the rustiest nail they could find. Huck climbed up on one of the stacks and jumped down onto the nail, driving it into his foot. Off he was whisked to the hospital, tetanus shot was given, fuss was made, ice cream was, in all probability, eaten. You will have to ask him if the pain was worth it!

Cabin—and camp living—is a zany mix of the mundane, the ridiculous, and the sublime. Kind of like any life authentically lived! In the second edition of the *Timberline Times*, Rocky focused his commentary on 'Redeeming the time.' He ends with the following, which I think is so much of what cabin and camp living teaches us about life overall:

Take time to think … it is the source of power.
Take time to play … it is the secret of perpetual youth.
Take time to read … it is the fountain of wisdom.
Take time to love and be loved … it is a God-given privilege.
Take time to be friendly … it is the road to happiness.
Take time to laugh … it is the music of the soul.
Take time to give … it is too short a day to be selfish.
Take time to work … it is the price of success.
Take time to do charity … it is the breath of heaven.

Here comes Jesus *(round as recorded by the Hall family)*
(sing through 3 times, raising key each time)

Here comes Jesus
See him walking on the water
He'll lift you up, and help you to stand.
Oh here comes Jesus
He's the master of the waves that roll
Here comes Jesus, he'll make you whole.

Jesus, is the way maker
Jesus is the way maker
Jesus is the way maker
He made the way for you and me
When the sun refused to shine
In this sinful heart of mine
Jesus, he made a way for me.
  (final time: He'll make you whole)

I think that this was one of Swede's favorite transition songs. I can recall him leading this song before chapel when campers were energetic and not yet in a chapel frame of mind, and I can remember him leading this song during campfire as he shifted from 'fun' songs into more serious songs. **Here comes Jesus** is the perfect blend of upbeat with a spiritual message. As campers, we could throw our energy into it, "**Jesus is the Way Maker!**" but it also began to center our thoughts on Christ.

4

Chapel

During my time at Timberline Ranch, 'chapel' was synonymous with 'Rocky.' Swede, though, held top billing, not only for music, but for entertaining and drawing campers in with puppets and magic acts that were sheer whacky genius. If something didn't quite 'work,' it became even funnier. Campers noisily would be gathering in the hotel basement, plopping onto mats and benches, chattering to each other, and Swede would begin to pull them into a cohesive gathering with his music or with Floop, the pink penguin. Within minutes they would be spellbound while he performed some feat of magic.

One TR staff alumnus recalls that many of the campers would be trying and trying to guess how Swede did things, while others would be completely drawn into the 'magic' of it. One camper became quite convinced that Swede could make King Tut appear from the tomb at will. True showman that he was, Swede never revealed his secrets!

Swede would, seemingly effortlessly, get the campers' unified focus, then would skillfully transition the campers from rollicking laughter to a relaxed group ready to receive Rocky's message.

Rocky wielded a wonderful gift. When giving a talk in chapel, he never spoke down to us. We heard the straight goods, whether it was stories about the war, about horses, or about his faith. Rocky had a vibrant walk with Christ that radiated from his fervent words and energetic voice and actions. I remember Rocky moving through his talks; he was never still, he acted out his words and we loved it. He was not above shouting when the story called for it! I do recall one time, some dozing campers (or were they staff?) jerking wide awake when Rocky yelled to Lazarus, "COME FORTH!"

Rocky walked and talked with a Bible in his hand. He usually had book themes for the camp week, and somewhere in a box of memorabilia, I still have the little book of Matthew that Rocky handed out to us at the beginning of one camp. On the cover was a picture of a flock of sheep in a green pasture. I also remember different weeks with the themes of the Psalms, Proverbs, and the Gospel of John. Rocky made alive the parables taught by Jesus. I still hear Rocky's voice when I read them.

One of my favorite chapel themes at one camp, though, was quite different. Rocky had a collection of large banners with the different dispensations of God's covenants with humankind. These were beautifully painted with illustrations of scriptural events. One week, Rocky brought these out and talked through them all the way from the Garden of Eden to end times. I remember the overarching words: God's Redemptive Plan. I was fascinated.

I had been raised in a Christian home so knew the individual scripture stories, but I hadn't grasped that 'big picture' so clearly before—this was past, present, and future brought to life right before me. A few years later, when Rocky invited our opinions on what chapel theme he should consider for an upcoming camp, I was able to tell him how much I appreciated his talks with those beautiful banners and 'vote' for these to be repeated. I can't remember if he took my suggestion that week, but I like to think he did!

After the hotel was built, chapels were usually held after lunch in the coolness of the basement. Before the advent of the hotel, chapels were held in, what was to become Candy's Cave, located in the bunkhouse; but Rocky often held chapel outside. One of our favorite places for chapel was the big rock where the ranch house now stands. That rock was the perfect place to hold chapel on a summer day. There were roughly cut-in steps up the rock, and soft moss and lichen to sit on. The universe felt so much closer. The view was great—you could see the bunkhouse below, and trees in every direction; the road snaked below from the horse pasture, past the bunkhouse, and out toward the big beams of the Timberline Ranch gate.

Rocky's voice was made for the open air. If anything, his animations and the rise and fall of his voice were even more energetic out under the blue sky. Swedie brought to memory for me the time Rocky was speaking on Elijah; he was living out the story of Elijah and the chariot of fire. Rocky was saying, "A chariot of fire and horses of fire came and took Elijah in a whirlwind!" Just as he said this, we heard thundering hooves below and saw a cloud of dust; the camp watched as Hoss, one the wranglers, went galloping down the road below and out the gate. Swedie called out, "Just like Elijah!"

We went to the big rock many times. Not only for chapel, but often we met with Rocky as a smaller group of counselors or staff, for prayer and morning devotions. The gospels seemed to take on a new reality to us there on that rock so much closer to heaven. I remember one such morning, Jinx exclaiming, "This is just what I imagine the disciples felt, sitting at the feet of Jesus and listening to him teach!" I was mildly horrified—thinking at once of the scripture where Peter blurts out that he wants to build three tents, one for Jesus, Moses, and Elijah! But deep inside, I knew just what she meant. What a privilege to be in that moment there on the rock, with this devoted follower of Christ and gifted teacher opening up for us his heart and mind. What a gift, now to look back and be there once again.

That big rock was an icon to us, meaning that truly it was a site that channeled our minds toward eternal things. Although we did our best to be happy for Rocky and Rockette when the new house was built over the rock, we were quite sad that we had lost 'our' spot. I remember cheering up a bit when Kermit showed me downstairs in the new house where you could still see sections of the rock, which really created a wonderful foundation for the Timberline house. Also, thankfully, there were two other big rocks at Timberline that were quite conducive to open air prayer meetings, so we weren't left totally bereaved!

Those big rocks at Timberline became 'chapel' even when only two or three of us met there. They were our places of prayer and contemplation. I have many memories of climbing to the top of the rock by the old cabins in the trees and praying wordlessly as I gazed into the blue sky. I also recall sitting on the rock with campers and staff and praying along with them as they opened their hearts to the love of Christ. I think that each time this miracle occurred, that sudden blossoming of mustard seed faith, I was somehow changed as well.

In my profession now as a nurse, I have provided care over the spectrum of life; during the birth and during the passing of a person from this life. Both of these events are always deep, core impacting moments for care providers who choose to be truly present with another and with THE Other. Those heart-prayers on the rock, years before at Timberline, had the same sensation of being on holy ground. Even though we were slapping mosquitos up there as the sun dipped and twilight settled in, nothing took that spirit of awe away.

Not even the humor that infused most Timberline events. One summer, Rocky held a Communion service for all staff and counselors beginning the camping season. There were about thirty or so of us, all grouped around the fire place in the hotel. I was seated between Jinx and Bean. We passed around bread and glasses of grape juice as Rocky read the scripture. I remember eyeing the large glass with trepidation, because I am a sipper who chokes easily—not a 'chugger.' Well, sure enough, when Rocky came to the part where we all ate and drank our symbols of the body and blood of Christ, although I tried desperately, I could not finish the juice in the minute time frame allotted before we moved into the hymn. I was mortified. I had to hold that glass through the rest of the service still with a quarter of the liquid in it. The minute the service was over, Jinx and Bean leaned forward simultaneously, staring me in the eye, "Drink ye ALL, Toby!" There is something about the holy that is never far from humor—at least when humans are in the mix!

Rocky often received letters from campers who told him how much chapel had meant to them. Sometimes he shared some of these stories in letters he wrote to the friends and supporters of Timberline. Here is one from a letter written in 1973:

> *"Hi, everyone, I am writing to you because I have gone through my first day as a Christian and have just read up to Gen. 9. I am most grateful for your hard work to turn me to Christ …"*

In the same letter, Rocky ends with a quotation by an unnamed author. It is a fitting ending for this piece devoted to chapel and those who served in this ministry at Timberline Ranch.

"I must walk close to youth. I must be true and earnest that I can counsel them. I am resolved that I shall give much thought and effort to help youth choose wisely, heroically and earnestly the path they are to take. Be this my one great aim—to counsel lives at the parting of the ways."

What a beautiful, wonderful day / Do you love Jesus
(medley & round) (as recorded by the Hall family)

What a beautiful, wonderful day
What a beautiful, wonderful way
To walk with my Lord, to talk with my Lord
What a beautiful, wonderful day!
There's nothing that I'd rather do
There's no place that I'd rather be
Than to walk with my Lord, to talk with my Lord
What a beautiful, wonderful day!

Do you love Jesus?
Jesus loves you,
Yes, I love Jesus,
and pray you love him to!

I remember Swede opening chapel with this song. I don't think I'll ever forget him strolling to the front of chapel in the hotel basement, strumming his guitar and leading us into the song. (Do you remember those blue mats we sat on?) This song is one of my favorites, and it was great to hear it again when I listened to Swede and Swedie's, **The Songs we Sing** album, where the whole family sings the medley.

Goliath of Gath (unknown author?)

Goliath of Gath, with a helmet of brath
was theated one day on a patch of green grath
Along came young David, a thervant of Thaul
and thaid, "I must thmite thee
although I'm tho thmall."

Goliath thaid, "Thonny, I'm bigger than you
tho don't you get funny or too bad for you.
David thaid, "No! Bye bye you must go"
With that he let fly, and he hit him in the eye.
He picked up hith thword
 when he thought he was dead

and lifted it up high, and cut off hith head.
He picked it up gently and thaid with a thcream,
"Why, poor old Goliath . . . you thure need . . .

Brylcream, a little dab'l do ya
Brylcream, you look so debonair
Brylcream, the girlth will all purthue ya
They love to run their fingerth through your hair!"

We would bug and bug Jinx to sing this song every camp. I can remember her lifting her famous hat every time she sang the line, 'with hith helmut of brath!" Everyone loved this song—except maybe Swede. Jinx's eyes would start to wander just before the 'Brylcream' part of the song. She would pick out some guy with neatly combed hair, run for him and, during the very last line, destroy his 'cool' hair by franticly running her own fingers through it. I have a suspicion that Swede was always worried that it was going to be him! (and sometimes it was!)

5

TR Camp Activities

The bell rang and we knew it was time to move onto the next activity of the day. For me and my group, that day back in 1969, it was riflery, so I began the walk from the Timberline workshop where archery was stationed, at that time, to the riflery range right at the back of the ranch. That Thursday, it seemed a comparatively long walk; the sun blazed down on us, making up time for all those rainy days we had experienced at the start of the week. I was eager to get some good shots in because for once I stood a chance at placing in riflery.

As my cabin mates and I walked through the buttercups and grass in the horse pasture, we saw the small cloud of dust from the horse corral. I briefly wondered who was riding Princess and if they were being kind to her sensitive mouth and nature. As we walked, we kept an eagle eye out for a few blackberries that hadn't been snagged yet by other campers. The blackberry vines were lush and buzzing with bees.

"Whoa," I exclaimed, jumping, startled by a small red-backed garter snake that lay still in the heat, like someone's forgotten belt. I had almost stepped on it. My friends only gave a half-pause in their conversation as they carefully stepped around it; we were already well used to these harmless, but startling little snakes in the pasture.

At the riflery range we took turns shooting the .22 caliber rifles at our small paper targets. When our five target shots were made, we took turns at shooting pop cans that were lined up along the posts and rail that held our targets. I remember being pleased with my target, printing my name on it, and handing it in to the counselor who was in charge of riflery. It baffled me that I was completely erratic with a bow and arrow at hitting the large archery target, but for some reason, quite consistently 'decent' at shooting rifles. The Timberline bell rang again and this time we pelted out of the coolness of the riflery station and into the pasture. It was our turn at the barn.

Riding at the barn was the highlight of the morning for most of us horse-crazy kids and we didn't want to miss a minute of it. I lined up outside the corral rails and waited for the wrangler to assign me to a horse. I was hoping it would be Princess, my current love, given that my friend had 'bumped' me off Topsy. My friend as given Topsy, but this time I got Dusky. Everyone looked at me pityingly. The wrangler noticed my slightly crestfallen look and said, "You can do it, Dusky's a good ride." Buoyed up by encouragement from one of my wrangler-heroes, I entered the corral, went to Dusky and patted her, wanting to make friends with her before putting the reins around her neck and swinging up into the saddle.

Dusky was slightly smaller than Princess; she and I were probably an ideal match at the time. Dusky was a lovely dun color; where most duns are somewhat dull, Dusky's coat shone. I turned Dusky, who neck reined beautifully, to enter the lineup and followed the horse in front of me. I remember doing my best to keep a horse length away. Dusky suddenly whipped around and bared her teeth at the horse behind her. "Sorry!" I heard my friend say. "I got too close!" Typical Dusky behavior and why she was not a favorite of campers.

In hindsight I realize that Dusky was quite the philosophical mare. She was very particular about who was in front of her and who was behind her and held precise and strong beliefs about the distance that other horses should be allowed near her. She was a horse that understood personal boundaries and was not afraid to speak her mind when other horses strayed from her own particular philosophy and understanding of these boundaries. It was nerve racking for a young rider!

I took a good grip, sat deep in the saddle and moved Dusky on with my heels. She went forward obediently, having spoken her piece to the negligent mare behind her (I think it was Shadow), and off we went down the road and into the far pasture below the rifle range. Our wrangler took us into the flat pasture and began a slow lope in a large circle. Dusky broke into a canter and within two strides I had a grin on my face. Dusky had a lovely floating gait, well worth the occasional sudden arguments with other horses that ventured too near her. It was a lovely ride that morning.

The Timberline bell chimed out just as we returned to the corral. Time for campers to head to the dining room for lunch. Off we went in twos and threes down the road toward the bunkhouse. I saw Jinx and her cabin mates link arms and begin to chant:

One! Two! Three! Four! Five! Six! Seven! Eight!
We. Are. A little bit crazy!

The *'We are a little bit crazy'* group walk was classic Jinx.

We lined up like statues in our cabin rows outside the bunkhouse, hoping that Swedie would see how straight and perfect our line was and let us into the dining room first. We were second in, but well pleased anyway.

By the way, that year at camp I got third in Riflery. I still have my Timberline Riflery crest!

In the first few years of Timberline camps, following breakfast and chapel, the morning activities were riding, riflery, archery, and camp craft. After lunch was rest period, cabin cleanup, and an afternoon activity. If the weather was good, the afternoon activity was swimming in the Alouette River. The truck was packed with campers and counselors and we headed out to the river for swimming and 'shooting the rapids' on inner tubes. I remember turning rocks over in the river and finding small crayfish. The sun dappled, fresh-running water was so welcome after the dust of the ranch morning activities.

Swede and others acted as life guards. Swede recalled for me many rescues that he made in Junior Girls camps. He told me that in one camp he had to pull three kids out in two days. I think (hope!) that was a record that has never been repeated. I personally remember a time Swede jumped in and pulled out a girl who had worn her jeans and tee shirt into the water and the weight dragged her down. Swede seemed to have a sixth sense about where he needed to be!

All but one activity group went swimming in the afternoon. Groups cycled through the week for an afternoon trail ride; when it was your group's turn, you stayed at the ranch and headed for the barn.

During the afternoon trail ride, Rocky astride Patches or Pepper would take us up into the Timberline hills, through the trees along part of the trail that we took to Goose Lake every Wednesday. Sometimes, Rocky would take the horses down to the river instead. Princess was a swimmer! What a wonderful feeling of being gently 'bucked' through the water. The horses all enjoyed themselves and went a little crazy with joy. Some wildly pawed the water and the swimmers shook themselves like big dogs as they emerged from the river; the horses jumped into a gallop as they hit the road. They would be nearly dry by the time we got back to the ranch.

Between our swimming time or our trail ride and the evening meal, we had counselor hunts, scavenger hunts, balloon stomps, skit night, and other games. When the weather wasn't so good for stretches at a time, Rocky and the camp program directors often came up with some very innovative afternoon activities. I remember one time Rocky loading the entire camp onto a school bus and taking us to Harrison Hot Springs. I also remember Swedie organizing popcorn parties with a 'horse' movie.

Pillow fights were very much a Junior Boys event and highly useful in working off some of the little-boy energy. Everyone dreaded boy's camp rest period. The campers were supposed to have a quiet hour before doing cabin clean up. Often they would be climbing the walls, bugging each other, doing everything but resting. One counselor came up with the brilliant idea to have a giant pillow fight out on the lawn just before rest period. The whole camp got into it and everyone was having a great time. Except one camper, who apparently got his feelings hurt by getting whacked in the face with a pillow. Well the next thing Chips saw, was this little guy, red-faced and furious, filling up a pillow case with sticks and rocks, saying, *"I'm going to get him! I'm going to get him!"* That was the end of the pillow fight.

Skit nights were, and I think probably still are, a ranch tradition that everyone looks forward to ... watching! Thankfully, many campers and counselors really enjoy performing, too. In fact, one counselor and staff member, Kermit, has made a professional career out of performing in the theatre, so who knows where Skit Night may lead to?

When I was first a camper, Skit Night was held outside. Before the Timberline house was built, the audience of campers and staff sat on the big rock facing the little house. The performing cabin would prepare behind the house and then take the 'stage' in front of the rock, with the house as a backdrop. Later, when the hotel was built, Skit Night moved inside to the basement.

The skit *'Pencils, Pencils!'* that Nik and Chips became known for was a classic. Other favorite skits became standard Timberline entertainment. For example, it seemed that at every camp, one cabin always did the skit where a row of campers sat, covered to their necks with blankets, and a second row of campers, hidden by the blanket, sat behind them with just their arms sticking out. It looked as though their arms belonged to the row of campers in front. The campers would then 'prepare for their day,' combing their hair, brushing their teeth, and washing their faces, all done blindly on them by the campers behind them, under the covers. The wildly ineffective arms coupled with the facial grimaces and unlikely comments made in an effort to steer the arms was always fun to watch.

Another old favorite was *'The Enlarging Machine.'* Campers would hold up a blanket or cardboard made to look like a machine and other campers who needed something bigger would throw an item into the machine. Out would fly a larger item; for example, a little pillow would be thrown in and a big one would come out of the machine, a tiny top would be dropped in and an oversized tee shirt would come out. At some point the machine quits working and the campers get very upset with it. Finally, one camper, in a fit of fury, spits into the machine—and gets a bucket of water in the face. Big laughs!

Another standard skit was of a movie director, often a counselor, directing a 'movie' during a terribly dramatic scene that just wouldn't come out right. The director would yell, "Cut, cut!" and then ask the actors to speed up the scene, slow down the scene, speak more loudly, and so on. The innovations and personalities involved always made these 'stand by' skits fun.

One of my favorite memories of a Skit Night is when Nik and I dressed up like hillbillies and wandered into the middle of the program, leading a goat and a chicken and improvising a sad conversation which led into us singing,

"Where oh where, are you tonight?
Why did you leave me here all alone?
I searched the world over and thought I found true love.
You met another and phuft you was gone!"

Silliness reigned on skit nights, and it was tremendous fun for campers to reverse the tables on counselors, directors, and wranglers by getting them involved as innocent participants in semi-embarrassing situations. I think that I have deliberately put out of my mind many of these moments! I do remember, however, a more gentle ribbing targeting Jinx by Odz.

Earlier that week, Jinx had told a few of us that when she and her dog had gone out for an morning walk on what looked like a promising morning, she had been disappointed by a large raindrop that smacked her on the face. Jinx didn't find out until after, when she was standing in front of her bathroom mirror, that it hadn't been a rain drop at all. She faintly recalled the caw of crows overhead as she saw reflected in her mirror the 'gift' they had dropped from above on her nose! Odz created a one person sketch immortalizing the event (actually, I think it was two person; a camper acted out the part of the dog). Funnily enough, I saw this little skit performed again when I visited Timberline years later! Has it become a classic?

The most gross memory I have of skit night is that one daring skit that one counselor a year would get his or her cabin to perform. I am quite squeamish, so I could not watch, especially the last part. I am compelled to write it out here, though, maybe to try to exorcise the memory of it from my brain. It starts out innocently enough, with a table, a towel, a glass of water, a tube of toothpaste, and a toothbrush. A camper breezes in and says, "What a great day! I better get ready for breakfast!" He or she then proceeds to brush their teeth with the toothbrush and glass of water. When he is done, he leaves. The next camper enters, says roughly the same thing, and proceeds to brush his or her teeth, with the same toothbrush and same glass of water. Oh, my, it goes on like this until every camper from the cabin has brushed their teeth. The last camper, or the counselor, drinks the water. I couldn't watch. There was a similar disgusting one about cabin-shared bubble gum stuck on a bunk bed post that I will leave to your imaginations.

Sometimes skit night became fashion show night for the Junior Girls. Each cabin would create fashion masterpieces out of toilet paper and then present these down a runway. Some of the cabins were very innovative! I think that Rockette, who was very budget minded was always a little horrified by the amount of toilet paper used.

Activities, such as skit nights and afternoon games required a lot on initiative and creativity but not so much capital as the main event at Timberline: the horses. Riflery and Archery were certainly less resource-heavy, and Rockette believed that canoes would be as well. I believe that it was a few years before canoes came on the scene at Timberline. I remember Rockette had wanted canoes for some time; I have firmly etched in my mind a picture of her throwing up her hands and uttering one word, "Canoes!" whenever there was a problem with a horse or something was needed at the barn. Rockette well recognized that canoes did not need to be fed year round and never needed vet visits or shoeing.

At first, canoes were rented for an occasional afternoon activity only, but as the years went on became part of the routine program for campers. For the first part of every summer, canoeing was an easy thing to do at Timberline because of the annual spring flooding. We could quite literally canoe from the ranch gate to the river and down the Alouette. I remember as a counselor hiding in a canoe along the edge of the swamp during a Counselor Hunt. Only a few campers found me, but plenty of mosquitos did!

When things dried up, though, canoeing at Timberline became more difficult and the canoes had to be transported to the river bend. Eventually, the Timberline canoe 'port' was dug out so that canoes could be taken from the canoe hut out to the river regardless of the flood situation.

The annual Timberline flood perhaps is the richest source of stories and memories for campers and staff alike. Campers had to be loaded onto a truck and driven through the flood to the ranch. Registration would occur on the closest dry road; parents would say goodbye to their kids and watch them disappear onto the back of a truck through the flood.

Chips recalled this and shook his head, wondering aloud at the trust these parents had in Rocky and the ranch, although he remembers the occasional parent phoning, asking if their child made it to the ranch okay. On the other hand, campers often experienced this trip on the back of a truck through the flood as the first activity of camp!

Not so the staff. It required a lot of planning to get necessary items in and out of the ranch. It also took ranch-toughness; I recall Rockette telling me about driving through the flood and glancing down and seeing little minnows swimming around her ankles!

Chips learned to drive the Timberline truck through flood water and recalls that there was a dip at the front gate that 'got' every newbie. Driving through the water you learned that once you started, you couldn't stop: "You'd get that wave going in front of you, if you slowed down, especially through the dip, the wave would wash back and over the engine."

Rocky was always optimistic about the flood and traveling back and forth from the dry roads to the ranch. A Timberline truck was kept on one side of the flood and another at the ranch. There were boats to move between the two when necessary. In fact, it was very necessary when Swedie was pregnant with her youngest daughter and had to go to and fro for doctor's visits and one very important trip to the labor and delivery room at Maple Ridge Hospital.

Often when Curly was program director for Junior Boys, the flood would be at its height. Chips was working at the ranch during one of these flood-rich summers and recalls this story.

It was registration day for Junior Boys. Curly looked at the water and wanted to use the boats to transport campers and their luggage to the ranch. Rocky was sure it would be fine to take the truck. Curly said again, "Let's use the boats." Rocky said, "Nah, let's take the truck." One more time, Curly looked at the water, then at Rocky, and said, "Let's use the boats." Rocky said breezily, "No, no, let's take the truck." They loaded up the campers, along with their sleeping bags and suitcases and pillows and other gear, and started down the flood-covered road. They reached the front gate, hit that dip in the road, and the water sloshed back into the engine. Rocky opened the door to see the flood level and in rushed the water—to their knees. "Dog Biscuits!" exclaimed Curly, "Dog Biscuits! I told you we should have used the boats, Rocky!" Chips looking back, saw suitcases and pillows beginning to float out over the water ... of course, the Junior Boys saw this as a great adventure!

The gravel roads full of potholes, water, and resulting mud often were defining descriptions of Timberline at the time. Sadly, Swede's earliest recollection of the ranch in 1965 was the rough road it took to get there! Thankfully, his second memory was his first Timberline campfire.

Chips says he still meets people who think Timberline is nothing but dirt: "We'll run into campers and missionary families from the '70's and all they remember is the mud hole before the hotel was built—'Oh, that Timberline is so muddy!' 'Well, when were you last there?' 'Oh, 1970 or so.' The kids remember the mud with fondness, the parents, otherwise!"

Typical of the ingenuity of camp program directors, the flood and mud situation spawned, not just a lot of frogs, but a longstanding tradition at Timberline for mixed teen camps: British Bulldog on Monday nights—in the mud. There is something about getting filthy dirty that 'levels' a group. Nobody can be a snob with mud on her face!

Nik and Chips recall this story:

One camper arrived with elaborate hair, nails and make up. She had newly bleached lint-blond hair. She went down to watch the others play British Bulldog, but was adamant that she was not into this kind of thing. Well, she watched as camper after camper became thoroughly covered with greasy, thick swamp mud. Her friends, mud-streaming down their faces, looked at each other, looked at her, at each other, then at her shining white hair. They picked up handfuls of mud and began lobbing them at her. Within seconds she was in the mud playing British Bulldog with the best of them!

Yes, while others learned to make lemonade when they were given lemons in their lives, we at Timberline learned to make mud into memories!

That swamp mud, though, did not rely on memory alone for it to stick around. That thick, greasy mud was silt and clay and when it was in your clothes was next to impossible to get out. Everyone got hosed down after British Bulldog, but much of that mud made its way back home. I'm sure, as mothers unpacked suitcases, for a few moments, Timberline was most likely NOT thought of very kindly!

Camp is synonymous with fun, activity, and the outdoors. At Timberline, camp activities filled our day, and our day was set in the rhythm of country living. Camp activities, however were much more than fillers and baby sitters. They provided the matrix of minutes from which grew the precious process of connection, of relationships, of presencing with one's self and another. Done in the heart of nature and natural life, TR activities provided an unfiltered medium to hear the Creator at the doorway of your own heart.

Isn't it great to be a Christian

Isn't it great to be a Christian,
isn't it great, isn't it great?
Isn't it great to be a Christian,
isn't it great, isn't it great?
Well if you'll agree with me,
then let's all say, 'Amen!' (AMEN!)
Isn't it great to be a Christian,
isn't it great, isn't it great!

Isn't it great that God's our Father...

Isn't it great that we're forgiven...

Isn't it great we're bound for heaven...

"Well if **YOU'LL** agree with **ME**..." You had to point at **YOU** and then at **ME** when Swede led this song. I remember this being a favourite in breaking down barriers between people. A great icebreaker, as counselors went out of their way to point wildly at each other, early in the week. Then, as the week progressed, campers began to better understand the song and its meaning. As campers came into personal knowledge, they would begin pointing and grinning ... a feel-good warm-up song! Thanks, Swede, for this and many, many other song memories!

Doo Whacka doo round

Doo whacka doo whacka doo whacka doo
whacka doo whacka doo whacka doo …
Boom, boom, boom,
Doo whacka doo whacka doo whacka doo
whacka doo whacka doo whacka doo …
Boom, boom, boom,
Doo whacka doo whacka doo whacka doo
whacka doo whacka doo whacka doo …
Boom, boom, boom,
Doo whacka doo whacka doo whacka doo
whacka doo whacka doo whacka doo …

(by unknown?)

Oh my mother and father are Irish,
My mother and father are Irish,
Oh my mother and father are Irish,
So I am Irish too … oh …

Sing to me a simple melody
One my mother sang to me
One with good old fashioned harmony
Sing, oh sing that song to me … oh …

Traditionally, this song was sung by counselors on banquet night. The timing had to be just right; the counselors stood in a row, linking arms, and every second counselor had to bop at the same time. Many of us were rather dance-challenged, having grown up in conservative Christian homes; so believe it or not, we had to work to get that alternate bopping going!

Sweet Violets (by unknown?)

There once was a farmer who took a young miss
in back of the barn where he gave her—
a lecture on horses and chickens and eggs,
and told her that she had such beautiful—
manners that suited a girl of her charms.
A girl that he wanted to take in his—
washing and ironing, and then if she did,
they would get married and raise lots of—

> Sweet violets, sweeter than all the roses.
> Covered all over from head to toe,
> Covered all over with sweet violets.

The girl told the farmer that he'd better stop,
or she'd call her father and he'd call a—
taxi that got there before very long,
'cause someone was doing his little girl—
right for a change and so that's why he said,
"If you marry her, son, you're better off—
single, for it's always been my belief,
that marriage will bring a man nothing but—

The farmer decided he'd wed anyway
and started preparing for his wedding—
suit which he purchased for only one buck.
But soon he found out he was just out of—
money, and so he got left in the lurch
a-standing and waiting in front of the—
end of the story, which just goes to show
that all a girl wants from a man is his—

My favorite mem-
ory of this song was
when three of us (I
think me, Nik, and
Little Hoss), dressed
up as daisies with
these giant flower
faces and sang this
during a banquet
night. To be scru-
pulously honest,
though, I think we
found it funnier
than the campers
did … !

Old Hiram's Goat

Old Hiram's goat
Was feeling fine
Ate three red shirts (chomp, chomp, chomp)
Right off the line
'Hi' took a stick
And gave him a whack (whack, whack, whack)
And tied him to
The railroad track
The whistle blew (whoo, whoo, whoo!)
The train drew nigh
Old Hiram's goat
Was doomed to die
He gave three groans (groan, groan, groan)
In mortal pain
Coughed up those shirts (cough, cough, cough)
(repeat above, this time with sound effects in brackets)
And flagged the train!

This song requires specific instructions. Each line is sung first by the song leader, and then repeated by the group. The first time around, the song is sung in its entirety, EXCEPT for the last line. The second time around, the sound effects (in brackets) are added. Again, the sound effects are first done by the song leader and repeated by the group. After the sound effects round, finally the last line is sung. Whew! What a relief, that goat is alright!

6

Goose Lake

I woke up in my sleeping bag at Timberline, hearing a quiet knock on my cabin door. "Toby? You awake?" It was Jinx, the quintessential early riser. It was well before the wake-up bell for the campers; time for me to rise, quickly wash, and get to counselors' prayer gathering.

Wednesday was a special day at Timberline; it was Goose Lake day. Right after lunch we would meet as a camp, pick up the packs that the kitchen staff prepared for us, and hit the trail for the roughly three mile hike to Goose Lake. As campers (and as counselors, too), most of us wore our bathing suits under our jeans and tee shirts so that we would be ready to hit the water without much delay.

The Goose Lake trail began at the tree line of the ranch, behind the campfire circle. A deep stream and swampy area, full of skunk cabbage and bulrushes cut along one edge of the beginning trail. This would become the site of the old Timberline swimming hole, after it was dug out and the entry leveled a bit. The first part of the trail was a fairly steep grade, with rocks underfoot, and campers—and horses, when they were taken up the trail—looked forward to the comparatively level ground ahead. The trail wandered through huckleberry-rich bush and some older growth Douglas fir. There was a section of lovely dips and fallen logs that were wonderful to jog through and jump over, especially when on horseback! Also, there was a level area that was ideal for a cool canter under the overhang of those huge, fragrant cedar and fir trees.

As new growth and fallen trees are expected cycles of life, the trail required a lot of maintenance. Hiking to Goose Lake as a camper, I remember ducking under a couple of large trees fallen over the trail. I know these and many more falls must have been cut up and moved by hand by Rocky, various wranglers, and other volunteers, so that the horses could get through and campers could travel safely. Whenever the horses were taken up to Goose Lake, though, they were tied a short distance away, along the trail. We would hike in the rest of the way from that point, because the trail was narrow and more 'foot' than 'hoof' friendly. Also, there wasn't a clear spot for the horses right at the lake.

That morning I had eight Junior Girls in my cabin, and all were excited about the mysterious Goose Lake and the long hike in. Goose Lake had many tales and 'facts' associated with it that flew around camp that morning: Goose Lake is bottomless; no fish live in Goose Lake; the water is right from a glacier, it's freezing! Like most rumors and legends, these were based on a kernel of truth. In fact, Goose Lake is very deep with no gradient shoreline; it is of glacial origin and it is cold! The fish story, I think is probably a fish story! I personally don't remember seeing any fish jumping at the lake, but I do remember a lovely water snake swimming alongside me. I was amazed at the diagonal forward movement of the snake, with its little head sticking out of the water. It outdistanced me, of which, secretly, I was glad! As on land, snakes have a suddenness about them that Emily Dickinson in her poem got so right, all those years ago.

Goose Lake looked, and is, carved out of rock; a deep bowl reflecting the green of trees overhanging and the tangle of roots and vegetation cascading into the water and sending shoots up again. We used those roots and vines like a ladder in and out of the lake. Because Goose Lake was so deep with no sloping shore, campers were allowed in only in limited numbers, usually in activity groups. Swede, Jinx and others were on their alert as life guards.

Evidence to the glacial gouging nature of Goose Lake's origin, are flat rocks protruding from the depths of the lake, visible from the top of the rock overlooking the lake. These shallow rock tables are seen as areas of a lighter reflection of the green. The experienced, stronger swimmers loved swimming out to those shallow rock plateaus. I always felt it was a badge of honor to say that you swam out to the rocks and envied those who had the courage to do this. I never did! I remember hearing their voices echoing across the lake to where the rest of us sat on the lichen encrusted shoreline or swam closer to the knotted roots.

The first order of business for the staff, before the swimming began, was to collect water from the lake and drop in the water purification tablets. After these tablets dissolved, flavored drink crystals were stirred in as an attempt to hide the taste of the iodine in those tablets. It never quite worked, but at least we were safe! We built our campfire on the rock face along the shore and roasted wieners and marshmallows and made S'mores. Often we had chapel up there, and sometimes, for older campers, we had campfire and came back in the twilight.

Goose Lake held a special spot in providing the context for kids to experience moments of encounter with themselves, as they struggled up a rocky bank or persevered through fears to conquer Goose Lake and swim out to the rocks. It also provided many moments of relational encounters with staff and counselors. For new counselors, young staff, and older campers, it further allowed for moments of mentoring in servant leadership. As counselors we were privileged to learn from camp leaders, such as Swede and Swedie, not only about the nuts and bolts of leading, but the relational dimension of being leaders.

I remember a personal moment of learning when we set off down the trail back to the ranch, flashlights in hand. Spreading like wildfire up the line of campers came back the panicked message that someone had seen a bear. My personal reaction was to shush the rumor to stop fueling the wave of fear threatening to break—I could already hear tears and rising hysteria in some campers' voices. My way was to sternly shut it down. Instead, I heard Swede begin cheerful singing and that song spread.

We sang the whole way back; no bears—or tears—in sight. The beauty of the night forest was recaptured; the moment of fear encountered, realized, and redeemed. I seem to remember vaguely that that first song was about a bear, but I can't recall the actual song. I still wonder if there really was a bear out there that night ...

Not all the staff went up on these Goose Lake hikes. Even with campers gone, there was still a lot of work to do on the ranch, although I am very sure that the staff enjoyed the few hours of quiet in which to do their work. That said, staff were at Timberline because they loved working with kids. Swedie and Sunny told me how staff always had half an ear open for the returning camp, and that it was always a thrill to see the campers return. Before they saw the glow of

Goose Lake

flashlights bobbing down the trail, they would hear singing, or the chant, *"We need ice water! We need ice water!"* That was the sign to quickly set out the late snack for hungry campers in the Tuck shop lounge.

Somehow, after that hike to Goose Lake, after inhaling the green scent of forest and feeling bracing lake water on your skin, after staring up into the star-filled sky and feeling the awe of eternity captured in the hum of life all around you, somehow, things were different. I know that the song by Ralph Carmichael, *He's Everything to Me*, such a campfire favorite for so many years, was sung with a deeper, resounding truth after that Goose Lake journey:

In the stars His handiwork I see
On the wind he speaks with majesty ...

Till by faith I met Him face to face
And I felt the wonder of His grace
Then I knew that He was more than just
A God who didn't care who lived away up there ...
He's everything to me!

By Wednesday evening, the weekly miracle of softening of hearts would have happened. That night, in our cabins the night time conversations would be different. God and his angels were present, and we, as counselors and staff, were privileged to have a front row seat.

He changed my life

He changed my life,
Jesus changed my life,
and he can do the same for you. Yes!
He changed my life
Calmed the din and strife
He wants to be your Savior, too!

A little man

A little man walked up and down to see what
he could see in town (repeat)

He came upon a stylish place and entered in
with modest grace (repeat)

His purse, his pocket he drew hence and
found he'd only fifteen cents (repeat)

The bill of fare he looked into to see what
fifteen cents would do (repeat)

The only thing t'would do at all was one meatball (repeat)

He called the waiter down the hall and softly
whispered, 'one meatball' (repeat)

The waiter bellowed down the hall 'This person here wants one meatball!" (repeat)

The little man felt ill at ease and softly whispered, 'bread, sir, if you please' (repeat)

The waiter bellowed down the hall, "You'll get
no bread with one meatball!" (repeat)

But that's not so at Timberline, they feed you
plenty all the time! (repeat)

7

Of beans and banquets, hotdogs
and doughboys ...

I remember reading the Timberline brochure to my friend over the phone and being a shade dismayed to read that we were expected to bring dress-up clothes for banquet night. I hadn't intended to wear anything but jeans and my cowboy shirt, my bathing suit, and a tee shirt over that, the entire two weeks. I mean, after all, this was a ranch with horses and cabins in the woods. But here it was, Friday afternoon at Timberline and my cabin mates and I were dressing for the banquet and suddenly I was very thankful for my Sunday clothes, feeling the excitement in the air.

I barely recognized some of my tomboy compadres—mainly because I hadn't seen one or two of them before without a cowboy hat on their heads! Everyone looked so serious and stood like grownups in their cabin lines outside the dining room. I remember Swedie standing on the bunkhouse steps commenting how nice everyone looked. Under Swedie's notice, I was doubly glad for my special clothes!

The dining room, when we entered, was transformed by balloons and streamers and there was music playing. Cookie and the kitchen staff had prepared a special dinner for us. The aroma of roast beef and gravy wafted over us as we took our seats. We enjoyed every bite of the food and every minute of the special music by Swede and Swedie, hilarious entertainment by the counselors, thoughtful words by Rocky, and, of course, awards presentations. I carried that memory with me, the 'special-ness' of banquet night, and tried to maintain that feeling for the campers when I became a counselor.

Like most of us who were staff at Timberline, I worked various camp weeks as either a counselor, wrangler, or kitchen staff. Although all camp work is demanding, working in the kitchen is perhaps the most character building— I suppose that reflects on the individual, I can only speak about my own rather stretching experience! I remember the first week that I worked in the kitchen under Cookie, I think it was with Odz, I was blown away by the speed that was needed to get all the dishes washed and dried and put away in time to do kitchen prep and set the tables for the next meal. At that time, the only dishwashers in that kitchen were the human kind! I think Cookie despaired of me, but by the end of the week, Odz and I were drying dishes three at a time like pros and we managed the potato peeling machine like champions.

Timberline meals at that time were served family style, with bowls of food taken to the tables. Although cabins sat together and there were staff tables, often staff intermingled and sat with camper groups. I remember one time as a camper, Rocky joining us at our table. We felt honored. Food is such a component of camp life, for campers and for staff. I remember in the old kitchen in the bunkhouse loading the milk boxes with the rubber tubing into the dairy refrigeration unit. Necessary for the care and feeding of campers, but that little spot in the kitchen also was a hangout for staff needing a short break and a cool glass of milk.

Meals at Timberline were family in more than just serving style. I remember that women from the Alliance church and other members of the Timberline Women's Auxiliary, often bringing in preserves, pies and cookies, and farmers donating fruit, produce, and even meat.

The dining room was a cheerful, humming place with spontaneous songs and laughter. Grace was often sung as a round:

"For health and strength and daily food,
We give you thanks, Oh Lord"

Of course, this angelic moment (that is, 'angelic' when grace was sung by Junior Girls) quickly was shattered by fun and chatter.

The singing often continued, but moved from the sublime to the ridiculous:

"We are table number one, number one, number one,
we are table number one, where is number two?"

This song could go on for some time, depending on the size of the camp and was a little character-building in itself sometimes, depending on your current level of energy!

Heaven help you if you were found to have your elbows on the table:

"Mabel, Mabel, strong and able,
Get your elbows off the table!
This is not a horses' stable, but a first class dining table!
Round the table you must go, you must go, you must go,
Round the table you must go, you've been naughty!"

And, God forbid that you were late to a meal:

*"What we want is more punctuality, more punctuality,
more punctuality. What we want is more punctuality here
at Timberline.
Here at Timberline, here at Timberline.
What we want is more punctuality here at Timberline."*

When the meal was nearing its end, an inevitable sight was the camp program director, often with a clipboard, walking to the front of the room. The younger camps (Junior Girls and Boys) loved singing the song:

*"Announcements, Announcements, Announcements!
A terrible death to die, a terrible death to die,
A terrible death to be talked to death,
A terrible death to die!*

Announcements,

Announcements,

Announcements!"

The dining room was the gateway to many, many moments of connection, laughter, and conversation. But food, at Timberline, certainly was not limited to the great indoors. Timberline food traditions in the open air included Dairy Queen Dilly® Bars after every Sunday night camp-opening barbeque, S'mores with real Hershey™ bars at Goose Lake, and Swedie's doughboys!

In a nostalgic moment last summer, I introduced my husband to doughboys. He was under-impressed, but I was lost in memories and didn't mind the slightly-raw center! If you will recall, doughboys are made by cutting green sticks about as thick as your thumb and as long as possible, wrapping Bisquick® dough around the first six inches of the stick, and cooking it over a fire. When it is done, doughboys will be able to be cleanly pulled off the stick. I have yet to see one do that—there always seemed to be a doughy spot in the middle, but as campers, this never deterred us. (Ahh, maybe THAT is why they are called 'doughboys'?) Doughboys are best eaten the Timberline way, with butter and strawberry jam pushed down the hole. Ummm!

Tuck shop favorites in the early days were Mojos® and Pixie Stix®, because these candies fit everyone's budget. I remember seeing Rocky walking the roadway with resignation picking up Mojo® wrappers and empty Pixie Stix® tubes. They were all over the grounds, and as staff, we all picked up our share, too.

I have in my Timberline memorabilia box an old Tuck card with my 'ration' of 10¢ a day. Rockette has neatly initialed the card and drawn lines through each day that I indulged in a Tuck shop spree. Definitely, I was a Mojo® and Pixie Stix® girl! My favorite Mojos® were orange and strawberry and we could get three for a penny. Believe it or not, at the time of this writing, Mojos® are still available for sale— they and Pixie Stix® have made it into online nostalgic candy shops—but now they cost a whopping 15¢ each! Pixie Stix® are now 10¢ each—about 100 times what they cost us as Timberline campers.

Swede or Rockette made the run into Malkins, the local supplier of candy and other goods in the early years; Chips and others took that role on later. The Timberline kids loved to go on the run to Malkins; so much so that Levi, Swede's daughter, confessed to smuggling Huck in the backseat of their car one time when she was the only one allowed to go. They only made it part way there before Huck peeked out and was found. They all loved to walk through the aisles and see boxes and boxes of candies on display, but there was only so much room in the car. It must have taken real fortitude to shop with a budget at Malkins. Rockette-type fortitude!

Rockette had the unenviable, but essential job of ensuring that there were enough food supplies for the camp. This often meant a good deal of stretching of donor dollars. As Chips said, "Rockette always went after a bargain, and most of the time, she got it!" I can say from my heart that I never went hungry at Timberline, thanks to Rockette's bargain hunting and the kitchen staff's good cooking.

Rockette told me about how unprepared she was in those early years at Timberline. She and Rocky had never been to camp as kids, so everything was a 'first' for her. Initially, Rockette cooked for the retreat groups that came to the ranch, as well as the first Timberline camps. She said to me, "I had no experience cooking for groups, and here I was set to cook for a camp. I had no idea of quantities for shopping. A 5 lb bag of corn starch was a huge amount to me! I remember one time early on, getting a camp lunch of beans, opening up a giant can and setting this out. I thought this was lots! It wasn't. I opened another giant can. That was gone in a flash! I'll never forget the look on this boy's face who kept coming back to the kitchen counter, *'More beans, please!'"*

A funny story emerged one afternoon as Rockette, Candy, Chips, Nik, Jinx and I enjoyed Rockette's hospitality in their home at Pitt Meadows. We were appreciating a wonderful dinner cooked by Rockette and reminiscing about the ranch and the early days. The conversation turned to Rockette's bargain hunting and became a confession of sorts. Here is the story, as told to me that lovely afternoon:

Of beans and banquets ...

Always on the lookout for a bargain for the ranch, Rockette bought 18 gallons of orange drink syrup that was super concentrated. For every gallon, the kitchen staff had to dilute it about twenty times. A happy bargain? Yes and no, depending on who you talk to. But all agree on this: it was the orange drink that would not end. Chips and Nik frankly describe it in one word as: *"horrible!"*

Chips talked about going down to the basement again and again, each time hoping the bottles of orange syrup would be finally finished off, but no, there would always be yet another gallon. The day finally came, though, when the last gallon was brought up from the basement and finished off. A day of rejoicing—but cut short. "The next thing we knew, Rockette had bought a bunch more. Rockette interjects, "it was such a bargain!" "Well," Chips continued, "Under cover of darkness, we took every jug of the stuff and hurled it into the swamp!"

The story does not end there. A few years later when the swamp at Timberline was drained, the bottles resurfaced, still full of thick, orange syrup that would not die.

In true Timberline fashion, I will add one final comment to this story. The moral of this lesson is:

Numbers 32:23 *"... be sure your sin will find you out."*

Apples and Bananas

I like to eat (I like to eat) eight apples and bananas,
I like to eat (I like to eat) eight apples and bananas.

(repeat, each time substituting the vowel sound, such as 'ay' sounds
for a different vowel sound: ee, I, oh, u)

The Watermelon Song

You can talk about your apples, your peaches and your pears,
Your 'simmons hanging on the 'simmon tree,
But bless your heart, my honey, of all the fruit that grows,
That watermelon is the one for me.

    Oooohhhhhh, hambone am sweet (slurp!), chicken am good (slurp!),
    possum meat is very, very fine (ain't it so!)
    But give me, oh give me, I really wish you would,
    That watermelon hanging on the vine!
    (final chorus: That wa-ter-mel-on hanging on the V-I-N-E, V.I.N.E . vine!)

Oh see that watermelon, a hangin' on the vine
I wish that watermelon it were mine (it were mine)
The farmer must be crazy, he lacks a heap of sense
Or he'd never leave that melon on the vine!

The night I went to fetch it was on a stormy night
And the moon as yet had not begun to shine (begun to shine!)
But oh the farmer saw me and shot me through the fence
But I never left that melon on the vine!

Angels watching over me

All night, all day (do, do, do)
Angels watching over me, my Lord (An-gels!)
All night, all day
Angels watching over me.
(Final: Angels watching over me! Angels watching
over me!)

Now I lay me down to sleep
Angels watching over me my Lord
Pray the Lord my soul to keep
Angels watching over me (chorus)

8

Angels watching over me

Rocky often spoke with tangible thanksgiving and gratitude to God for the years of campers and staff coming on and off the ranch without any serious accidents. Many times campers, counselors and staff felt the presence of God and his ministering angels at Timberline.

While I am writing this, I'm seeing the vision of a careening stagecoach with Patches and, I think it was Gypsy Mare, galloping flat out, heading to 'safety' and the barn. The sight of two panicked horses dragging a tippy wooden box along a rough ranch road is not easy to forget. No one was hurt, either inside or outside the stagecoach, although I think that a few grey hairs sprouted on several heads that afternoon! There were many, many prayers of thanksgiving that day.

In the 1972 Timberline Ranch annual report, Rocky and Rockette recorded the following:

"Protection was granted us wonderfully. Over a 1000 children have camped at Timberline in the past five years. The Ranch activities of horsemanship, riding, riflery, archery and swimming have the highest accident ratios, yet we have had no serious accident among all those children."

The report goes on to list two accidents that resulted in a broken bone each (one leg and one arm), and "some bruised elbows and a lot of damaged egos from being tumbled off a horse."

As I was reading this careful listing of negative events delivered in the annual report, I was struck again by the simple authenticity that was expected of and delivered by Timberline Ranch. What a privilege to be mentored by this leadership that practiced truth telling and believed in miracles. The list continued and I read on:

"... and one boy lost in the woods but this had a happy ending. When the boy realized he was lost, he climbed a tree to see if he could find his way, and while up there, in repentance, asked God to forgive his sin. He later testified around the campfire that he was saved while up the tree, and came down a Christian."

The angels were busy in the forest that day!

There were many times that horses were suddenly calmed, or people felt 'pushed' to check something, go back into cabins, or look in a different direction, which in all likelihood changed the course of events for good.

Swede recalled for me the time that he had difficulty sleeping one night. Swede and Swedie and their family were living in the smaller ranch house at the time. Swede was restless. Unable to sleep, he was checking the house, and suddenly smelled smoke. He opened the front door and saw smoke and flames. Swede called the fire department who got there in time to put out what could have been a house-consuming fire. Apparently, there had been a bird's nest above the porch light that had been smoldering and finally burst into flames.

Another near-miss fire occurred in a cabin early one morning. The first cabins at Timberline were wood-constructed rustic structures with many of them set on stilts. They bordered the tree line above the horse pasture. Each cabin had a potbellied stove made from a 40 gallon drum and a stovepipe chimney that stuck out the roof. We loved the cozy, crackling warmth of those stoves when at camp in fall and early spring, or through prolonged rainy periods during the summer.

Well, one cabin loved their wood stove a bit too much, and loaded it to the extreme. Jinx, the early riser on staff, was walking by the cabin from the large rock behind the cabins were she had her morning devotions. The roof was smoking and the stove pipe was cherry red. Jinx yelled, "Fire!" and climbed up so that she could throw the buckets of water passed to her. Thankfully, the creek was close by.

Nik recalls running to spread the alarm to Swedie and Rocky and then being one of the bucket brigade. Miraculously, the roof did not ignite and no one was injured. The bucket brigade—especially Jinx—were heroes that day and have certainly earned a spot in Timberline history!

Ranch work in itself is not without risk, never mind dozens of campers, rifles, horses, bows and arrows, hiking, and water sports. Swede recounted the time that he and Matt were in the swamp through the height of the flood clearing brush for the boat to get through. They were sopping wet, working in water well over their knees, and a tremendous clap of thunder alerted them to huge storm clouds that had gathered overhead. There was no time to get to the boat and get out of there. The storm broke and lightning ripped across the sky, Swede all the while praying that a tree would not get struck by a bolt that would, inevitably, travel through the water. It was the worst thunder storm that Swede ever experienced at the ranch, yet that day Timberline—including Swede and Matt—was held safe in the 'hollow of His hand'.

Swede shared with me another story of a happening at Timberline that could have gone tragic. Swede and Swedie lived in various places at Timberline until they settled into what became known as the Timberline 'cottage' after the house on the rock was built. Before this they lived in the tiny house-that-doubled-as-a-nurses' station, then in the area of the hotel that would become the kitchen (they fashioned walls by hanging blankets), then down the hall from the offices, and their last stop in the hotel was upstairs, along the end of one hall. This story took place when they had just moved upstairs in the hotel.

As the hotel took shape inside and out, Rocky wanted some landscaping to be done around the hotel. For years there had been a muddy hole, and with construction ongoing, a lawn around the hotel was nearly impossible to grow. There was a huge stump behind the hotel that needed to be cleared in order for some beautification to take place, and, as Swede told me, "Rocky wanted it GONE!"

Swede and a few others worked on this project one afternoon before camping season was underway. Dynamite was often used to shift stumps, so that is what they used. To their horror, however, it was as though they shot off a cannon. Swede said, "The hollow stump acted like a gun barrel and blew rocks and mud right through the hotel wall." Meanwhile, Swedie was holding a Bible study in the hotel when the blast shook the hotel. Thankfully, all were safe, as they were upstairs in their new rooms. What a horror to go downstairs and see the debris blown right into what would become the dining room!

At the ranch there was no doubt that bigger things were going on than could be seen with the human eye. Looking up at the sky at night, stars shimmering and planets gleaming, watching the clouds scud across the moon, hearing the rain blown in waves over the cabin roof, you were called to feel the power of something greater than humankind. Feeling the steady welcome of the 'camp pillars,' the gleam of comradery in the eyes of fellow staff, and witnessing the softening and brightening faces of campers throughout the week, led you into the core-deep knowledge that heaven was a stone's throw away and that heavenly hosts stood all around.

When I was in Grade six, I talked about Timberline so much that six of my friends signed up for camp with me that summer. We were all in one cabin and we loved our counselor, who was called, I believe, Stripes. On Wednesday night, after campfire, one by one, everyone in the cabin met Jesus in a new way most personal and profound for her. It was an evening of rejoicing for us as we felt a bond that we had not felt before. Someone suggested, "Let's go tell Swedie!" and before you know it, out of the cabin we went in our nightgowns and pajamas and robes, across to the other grouping of cabins, knowing that Swede and Swedie did night rounds.

It was a lovely night with a warm summer breeze blowing thin clouds over a half moon—just enough light for us to see where we were going. We saw a flashlight in the distance and guessed that it was Swedie, so we quietly headed in her direction, not wanting to wake up the other campers. Sure enough, it was Swedie, who was happy to hear our news and walked us back to our cabin.

A couple of years later, as a counselor, I heard Swedie's perspective of that evening:

Swedie was tired. Wednesday was Goose Lake day and a long hike, 65 or so campers, and little sleep the last two nights had left her reserves on low. Swede was at the hotel taking care of their own children, but would be up to spell off Swedie for one later round of cabin checks. Swedie was heading for the last group of cabins to call out a quiet, 'Goodnight, cabin seven,' and then head back to the house for a well-earned rest. Suddenly, she saw in the distance, a small group of white robed figures, their clothes whirling around them like heavenly incense. Swedie stopped. Closed her eyes, and then opened them again. The messengers came nearer. "Not tonight, Lord," She silently prayed, "I'm too tired to meet angels." The white-robed messengers came on. Resigned to the will of the Lord, she walked forward to meet them.

Although I can safely attest to the fact that my cabin mates and I were not angels, I am aware that angels were present and made themselves known at Timberline on at least two different occasions in my time. I have a feeling that there are most likely many more encounters that others have had with angels at the ranch. I think, though, that most of the time these visits are personal and so specific to the person and moment that they are held sacred and not shared, or over time, questioned and forgotten.

Every summer that I was involved with Timberline Ranch, I can recall that there were small events and stories circulating of angelic interference for good. However, when interviewing people in preparation for the writing of this book, none of these stories emerged. I puzzled over this, wondering why people would forget these events or be reticent to share them.

Angels watching over me

I think there is something about spiritual encounters that transform us, but the glory, rightly so, goes to the Father. The mere situation, including the messenger, recedes and becomes only a vague memory; a backdrop to the Person Himself. When we do recall the messenger's visit, I believe, we are meant to for a reason. Because of this, I am recording the following two stories; one that was given to me to remember, and one that was given to my sister, Twiggy, also staff at Timberline, to remember. I am doing this because I believe that I was given these two memories for a reason, and a part of that reason is to share them with you:

It seemed, in Junior Girls, that the cabin, or cabins, of eleven year olds were always the most challenging. They were full of energy, mischievous, and tried to outdo one another. One year, Misty, a lovely counselor who was new to the ranch, was assigned to, what turned out to be, a challenging cabin of eleven year olds. Misty was an MK (missionary's kid) and I remember her as one of the most gracious and soft spoken women of heart that I've ever met. On Tuesday morning, at Counselors' Prayer Meeting, we prayed for Misty because she had had almost no sleep for the last two nights with these campers. After campfire, a few of us counselors noticed that Misty was in tears, not wanting to go back to her cabin. We stood in a group and prayed for her, while campers went off in all directions to their various cabins.

The next morning, we heard Misty's story. She had walked slowly back to her cabin, praying as she walked. As she neared it, she stopped, because it was silent. She wondered if the campers were playing a trick on her, or were possibly not even in the cabin but out wreaking havoc elsewhere! Misty walked up the stairs, opened the door and saw, by the light of her flashlight that each bunk was occupied by her campers. She asked them if they were all right.

"Oh," a girl said, "They've stopped."

Another girl said, "They're gone now."

Puzzled, Misty asked them what they meant. They told her that they had been listening to the angels singing. Nothing more, nothing less; that was the extent of their understanding and, in my recollection, they did not elaborate further. The angels, quite simply, were singing them to sleep.

The second story occurred one summer when we had had a couple of encounters with two young cougars. As far as I know, these cougars never approached any campers or threatened any ranch animals. However, Jinx had seen them sunning themselves on the roof of an unused cabin, and some staff, including me, had seen a quick tawny movement among the trees, and the reflection of eyes in flashlight beams at night when doing rounds. We knew they were out there. We had all heard the cougars call at night and it was a wild and eerie sound, although quite beautiful—when safe in your cabin!

During campfire that night, several campers felt that they were being watched by the cougars and the fear seemed to spread to many campers and some counselors. We always walked in groups with bright flashlights, so there was little actual danger, but knowing that cougars were quite likely around was more than a little disconcerting during those night walks from campfire to cabin.

Taps was sung that night, the night prayer was prayed, and counselors began gathering up their groups to walk back to the cabins. My sister noticed that a few of her campers had already left, so started walking with the majority of her group to their cabin in an effort to catch up with them along the way. They never did. When she got her group inside her cabin, she was relieved to see the three campers who had gone off by themselves safe and sound.

98

Angels watching over me

Twiggy asked them, "I thought you were afraid of the cougars? Weren't you scared to walk all this way by your-selves?" The campers told her that they weren't afraid because they had seen angels swirling around. "We just walked toward them." They did not describe in any more detail the angels to Twiggy, just simply, that they were angels and they were 'swirling.'

Timberline Ranch was covered in a mantle of prayer and God, I believe, many times sent angels, as the ancient prayer requests, *"in front of us, behind us, above us, below us, to our right, and to our left."*

"See, I am sending an angel before you, to guard you on the way and bring you to the place I have prepared." Exodus 23: 20.

Eutychus (by Ted 'Swede' Hall)

(background: Eutychus, Eutychus, Eutychus, Eutychus ..
Eu—ty—chus, Eu—ty—chus, Eu—ty—chus ...)

Eutychus fell out the window and he landed on his head,
Eutychus fell three stories, so Eutychus was dead.
Paul raced down the stairway, embraced him with his
arm,
God brought that boy back to life, saved Eutychus from
harm.

>   Saved Eutychus from harm,
>   saved Eutychus from harm,
>   God brought that boy back to life,
>   saved Eutychus from harm.

Paul had preached till midnight,
so Eutychus fell asleep,
He fell right out that window;
his sleep had been so deep.

Fire, Fire

(by an Ethiopian former witch doctor, arranged by Swede)

Fire, fire is my cry
And I need it till I die
I can feel the fire burning in my soul
When the old man is dead
Then the fire's sure to spread
I can feel the fire burning in my soul.

>   In my soul, fire, fire,
>   In my soul, burning, burning
>   I can feel the fire burning in my soul
>   When the old man is dead
>   Then the fire's sure to spread
>   I can feel the fire burning in my soul

9

Campfire

hinking back, I never remember the campfire actually being built and lit. The campfire simply existed, full burn, so to speak, for us as campers and counselors. My suspicion is that Swede got the fire going most times, but please forgive me if I'm overlooking your part in this!

In many ways, campfire was the pivotal point of camp. Even for me as a horse-crazy camper, I looked forward to campfire as the perfect capstone to the day. It fed my soul and my spirit. Somehow, guitar led songs and the glowing heart of a fire are welded together in the same way that blue sky is the perfect canvas for the brilliant green of a tree.

In August, 1973, Rocky wrote a letter to the friends of Timberline Ranch, summarizing the summer camp season, all in capital letters, as: "FRUITFUL, EXCITING, NOISY, THRILLING, HECTIC, HILARIOUS, BUSY, TEARFUL, and TIRING!"

I would suggest that, for staff anyway, campfire all by itself ran the gamut of those descriptives, and, I would add to the list, soul searching and spirit stirring.

A campfire song favorite that exemplified soul searching is the 1963 classic folk song by Bob Dylan, *Blowin' in the Wind*. The haunting refrain, *'the answer my friend, is blowin' in the wind, the answer is blowin' in the wind,"* seemed to sum up the baffling search for meaning that so many young people were going through in the 60's and 70's.

Swede wrote a final verse for *Blowin' in the Wind*, which captures the heart of the ministry of Timberline Ranch, and exemplified the spirit stirring activity of campfire:

> *These are all questions both deep and profound*
> *The kind that trouble my mind*
> *Yes and these are all questions that wise men for years*
> *Have tried the answers to find*
> *But the wise men have searched*
> *and will search again in vain*
> *For the truth they're searching for is not mankind's*
> *The truth and the way is found in Jesus Christ*
> *Yes the answer is found in Jesus Christ.*

Swede often led into *Blowin in the Wind* following another classic folk song of the 60's by Pete Seeger, *Where Have All the Flowers Gone*. Like *Blowin in the Wind, Where Have All the Flowers Gone* echoes King Solomon's, *"vanity of vanities, all is vanity …,"* leading to the king's defeated-sounding summation, *"… there is no new thing under the sun"* (Ecclesiastes 1: 2, 9).

Swede's answer to this deep angst for meaning was not to ignore or even reframe the questions, it was simply to point to the person of Jesus Christ. Timberline was not about creating adherents to a denominational church or creed, Timberline had what I see now as a winning combination. The Timberline 'pillars', men and women of God, respected the complexity of life and the questions generated in real living, honored the seeker in everyone, and steadfastly sought to walk in the love of God, as demonstrated by Jesus. It was simple and profound. It was powerful, and campfire radiated with it.

For many years, Swede and Swedie became synonymous for 'campfire' at Timberline. Swede's first experience of Timberline was at a campfire. Swede was in Vancouver in 1965 with the Billy Graham crusade. A Vancouver friend of his said, "You must see Timberline Ranch," and drove Swede and another crusade leader out to Timberline. It happened to be campfire time during a Navigators' camp. Swede just happened to have a ukulele with him, and joined right in. Swede's picture was taken along with the 'bigger name' crusade leader friend, and Swede found it amusing that the caption under those photos, published in Decision magazine, read, 'Unknown Ukulele Player' under his picture! Obviously, not in it for the fame, two years later Swede and Swedie had came to Timberline for their first full camping season at Timberline to lead the music. How wonderful for us!

Swede and Swedie never 'staged' a campfire. Swedie said to me that, "We went with how it felt: fun songs, to faster gospel songs and choruses, some solos interspersed with thoughts and testimonies, to slower gospel songs." To me, campfire always felt orchestrated in the best sense of that word; conducted with great sensitivity toward the things of the spirit, heart, mind and soul.

Campfire not only respected the seeker in everyone, it also honored the essential human-ness of people! Laughter, silly songs and jokes filled the air. The robust, scare-the-birds-out-of-the-trees song, *The Horse Went Around*, got the kinks out of any Junior boy. At least once every camp, Swedie's clear voice would ring out with, *"You should see our …. Odz! do the hula-la!"* and soon any inhibitions related to singing and moving your hips disappeared, *"Oh, wai, oh, hula-la!" The Hula-La Song* was a favorite of Junior Girls, who loved to put counselors and wranglers on the spot for a hula-la dance solo. Another favorite Junior Girl nonsense song, actually more of a chant that Swedie led was *Flea Fly*:

> *Flea*
> *Flea fly*
> *Flea fly flo*
> *Vista, coomalah coomalah coomalah vee vista*
> *Oh no no no not vee vista*
> *Eeny meeny decimeeny ooua loo-ala-meeny*
> *Acimeeny zalimeeny ooua loo-a-lah meeny*
> *Beat bilee od'en dod'en bo bo ber did'en dod'en*
> *Hush… …*

Yet another huge favorite warm-er-upper was the *Ostrich Song*. There is an ongoing debate among Timberline people about whether or not it is an *'Ostrich'* or an *'Austrian'* who is yodeling on that mountain top. I went through years at Timberline wavering from one side to the other, but am now firmly on the *'Ostrich'* side of the debate. Although I concede to the logic that Austrians do indeed hold histori-cal—and geographical—precedence for yodeling on mountain tops, I am of the opinion that, when viewed as an entire work of genius nonsense, the song makes more *non*sense with an Ostrich yodeler. My apologies to those of you who may side with the Austrian-as-yodeler school of thought; but I hum-bly ask you to consider the Ostrich-as-yodeler perspective as enriching the nonsense experience:

Campfire

Once an Ostrich (or Austrian) went yodeling on a mountain so high,
When along came a cuckoo bird, interrupting his cry
Oh, lay, oh …

yodelapiki a yodila cukoo, cukoo
yodelapiki a yodila cukoo, cukoo
yodelapiki a yodila cukoo, cukoo
yodelapiki cukoo

Once an ostrich (or Austrian) went yodeling on a mountain so high,
When along came a skier (swish!) interrupting his cry …

Once an ostrich (or Austrian) went yodeling on a mountain so high,
When along came an avalanche (rumble, rumble) interrupting his cry …

Once an ostrich (or Austrian) went yodeling on a mountain so high,
When along came a pretty girl (Kiss!) interrupting his cry …

Once an ostrich (or Austrian) went yodeling on a mountain so high,
When along came a St Bernard (yuck!) interrupting his cry …

I believe that I have made my point.

Another nature-defying favorite of Junior Girls was *'Alice the Camel has five humps.'* This is because they got to body check and bump each other at the end, "boom, boom, boom, boom!" Unfathomably, 'Alice' turns out to be a horse.

As campfire progressed, Swede, often with Swedie, sang songs that we joined in with or just listened to, such as *"The Wreck of Old 97"* where we did the train sound effects, *"Running Bear," "Kalidjah," "The Prisoner/There is Power," "I'll Fly Away," "Will the Circle Be Unbroken," "Daddy Frank,"* and *"Coat of Many Colors."* Swede expertly drew on songs that worked to transition from the nonsense-fun to the more thought-provoking and heart-tugging, sandwiching in songs that told a story between more action songs.

Some transition-type songs beloved of Junior Girls were, *"Father Abraham had seven sons, sir!"* and *"Noah built an Arky, Arky, Arky!"* These songs quickly led into *"His Banner, over me, is love,"* and *"Come to the Water."*

The campfire would be glowing now, a bed of deep coals with winking embers. Often, at this time a counselor or staff member would speak, sharing their spiritual journey.

Friday campfire was devoted to sharing by campers or any staff who felt led to say a few words. Each one would rise from where they were seated in the ring; from one of the logs, or from off the ground in front of a log where they had been leaning back into it. Cabin mates and camp friends would be listening earnestly, staring into the flames. The person sharing would reach out, pick up a stick, and say a few words about their camp experience, often speaking about their spiritual journey that week. They would then throw their stick into the flames and someone else would come forward to share. These shared stories were often very moving, deeply personal, and even soul-baring at times.

Dolly Parton, in her role as Truvy in the film, *Steel Magnolias*, says, "Laughter through tears is my favorite emotion." At Timberline, during the stick fire, we experienced a lot of that emotion! There is something about camp life that lends itself to ridiculous situations, yet these situations are often ones that reduce us to our authentic essence and allow us to open up to each other and to Christ.

For example, can you imagine sitting around the Timberline campfire, watching as a Junior Boy shifts from one foot to another, taps his open hand with the stick he has picked up, now clutched in a slightly grimy fist, screws up his face and begins to tell his story. He had wandered away from the others and had become lost in the woods ...

Campfire

Yes, you will recall this story from a previous chapter: the boy who went up a tree, repented, and came down a Christian. Like the biblical Zacheus, there is something here that is both heart-tugging and gut-splitting!

There is also the time, Swede recalled to me, that a small comedic-tragedy occurred in a Junior Boy's camp. Swede would often see some of the younger boys nodding off during campfire. One time, a little fellow with large cowboy boots was toasting his feet on a rock by the fire and slowly drifting off while listening to the singing, when Swede noticed steam rising off his boots. In the same second, a yell burst out of the boy, now fully awake, and he jumped to his feet, and then very quickly sat down again. His counselor and others helped pull off the boy's boots that indeed had become very toasty! *Fire, fire is my cry!*

In 1997, I had the opportunity to meet with Swede and Swedie and ask about their thoughts on campfire. From Swedie's perspective as camp program director for many years, campers and counselors saw campfire as a highlight of the Timberline experience: "the kids remember campfires, and counselors see it as the time to draw things together." They talked about the effort to maintain campfire up in the Timberline fire ring. Every year there would be a struggle to get fire permits for the camping season. Every year but one they received their permit; that one year, they held campfire in the hotel basement fireplace. I was staff that year and recall those campfires in the hotel. Amazingly, what I do not recall is a sense of loss or an attitude of doing things 'second best'. I remember wonderful campfires full of meaning.

That evening in 1997, I had the unforgettable experience, once again to participate in a campfire at Timberline with Swede. Swedie, Curly and Curlette, Rusty and Sunny,

Jinx, Nik and Chips were there. Curly, as usual (according to Swede!), kept throwing more and more wood on the fire, and Jinx and I kept remembering songs and asking Swede, for "just one more!" a few dozen times. What a gift, and I am grateful for that special memory.

Taps

Day is done.
Gone the sun;
From the lake, from the hills, from the sky.
All is well;
Safely rest,
God is nigh.

Good night, campers!

IT IS WELL WITH MY SOUL (D Flat)

When peace, like a river, attendeth my way,
When sorrows like sea-billows roll;
Whatever my lot, Thou hast taught me to say,
"It is well, it is well with my soul."

Chorus:
It is well, with my soul,
It is well, it is well with my soul.

And, Lord, haste the day when the faith
shall be sight,
The clouds be roll'd back as a scroll;
The trump shall resound, and the Lord shall
descend,
"Even so" it is well with my soul.

JUST AS I AM (E Flat)

Just as I am, without one plea,
But that Thy blood was shed for me,
And that Thou bidd'st me come to Thee,
O Lamb of God I come! I come!

Just as I am Thou wilt receive,
Wilt welcome, pardon, cleanse, relieve;
Because Thy promise I believe,
O Lamb of God I come! I come!

LEANING ON THE EVERLASTING ARMS (A)

What a fellowship, what a joy divine,
Leaning on the everlasting arms;
What a blessedness, what a peace is mine,
Leaning on the everlasting arms.

Chorus:
Leaning, leaning,
Safe and secure from all alarms;
Leaning, leaning,
Leaning on the everlasting arms.

What have I to dread, what have I to fear,
Leaning on the everlasting arms?
I have blessed peace with my Lord so near,
Leaning on the everlasting arms.

MY LORD KNOWS THE WAY (F)

My Lord knows the way thro' the wilderness,
All I have to do is follow.
My Lord knows the way thro' the wilderness,
All I have to do is follow.
Strength for today is mine all the way,
And all I need for tomorrow,
My Lord knows the way thro' the wilderness,
All I have to do is follow.

ISN'T HE WONDERFUL (B Flat)

Isn't He wonderful, wonderful, wonderful,
Isn't Jesus my Lord wonderful?
Eyes have seen, ears have heard,
It's recorded in His word,
Isn't Jesus my Lord wonderful?

HEAVENLY SUNSHINE (D Flat)

Heavenly sunshine, heavenly sunshine,
Flooding my soul with glory divine;
Heavenly sunshine, heavenly sunshine,
Hallelujah! Jesus is mine!

COUNT YOUR BLESSINGS (E Flat)

When upon life's billows you are tempest
tossed,
When you are discouraged, thinking all is
lost,
Count your blessings, name them one
by one,
And it will surprise you what the Lord hath
done.

Chorus:
Count your blessings,
Name them one by one;
Count your (many) blessings,
See what God hath done.
(Repeat entire chorus.)

So, amid the conflict, whether great or small,
Do not be discouraged, God is over all;
Count your many blessings, angels will
attend,
Help and comfort give you to your journey's
end.

ARE WE DOWN-HEARTED? (F)

Are we down-hearted? No! No! No!
Are we down-hearted? No! No! No!
Troubles may come and troubles may go,
We trust in Jesus, come weal or woe,
Are we down-hearted? No! No! No!

I BELIEVE THE ANSWER'S ON THE WAY! (D)

I believe the answer's on the way;
I believe the Lord has heard me pray;
"Cast not away your confidence,"
Saith the Lord our God.
Now by faith in Him alone I stand,
Firmly held by His almighty hand;
Fully trusting in His promise,
Praise the Lord!

HE OWNS THE CATTLE ON A THOUSAND HILLS (C)

He owns the cattle on a thousand hills,
The wealth in ev'ry mine;
He owns the rivers and the rocks and rills,
The sun and stars that shine,
Wonderful riches more than tongue can tell,
He is my Father so they're mine as well;
He owns the cattle on a thousand hills,
I know that He will care for me.

GONE, GONE, GONE, GONE (C)

Gone, gone, gone, gone!
Yes, my sins are gone.
Now my soul is free, and in my
heart's a song;
Buried in the deepest sea,
Yes, that's good enough for me;
I shall live eternally,
Praise God! My sins are gone!

BLESSED ASSURANCE (D)

Blessed assurance, Jesus is mine!
Oh, what a foretaste of glory divine!
Heir of salvation, purchase of God,
Born of His Spirit, washed in His blood.

Chorus:
This is my story, this is my song,
Praising my Savior, all the day long;
This is my story, this is my song,
Praising my Savior all the day long.

Perfect submission, all is at rest,
I in my Savior am happy and blest;
Watching and waiting, looking above,
Filled with His goodness, lost in His love.

Turn your eyes upon Jesus

(by Helen H. Lemmel, 1918)

O soul, are you weary and troubled?
No light in the darkness you see?
There's life for a look at the Savior,
And life more abundant and free!

    Turn your eyes upon Jesus,
    Look full in His wonderful face,
    And the things of earth will grow strangely dim,
    In the light of His glory and grace.

Through death into life everlasting
He passed, and we follow Him there;
Over us sin no more hath dominion—
For more than conquerors we are!

His Word shall not fail you—He promised;
Believe Him, and all will be well:
Then go to a world that is dying,
His perfect salvation to tell!

10

Upon this rock

I will never forget sitting in chapel one sunny morning, listening to Rocky talking about heaven. As I've said, Rocky always had an animated way of speaking and his words flowed from his heart.

"When I get there," he said, "one of the first things I'm going to do is make a big sign, 'TIMBERLINE CAMPERS, THIS WAY! So we can all get together. We'll have a big reunion up there!" I think that for many of us, our thoughts were, *Wow! The perfect Timberline Ranch Camp that would never end!* Rocky had a way of making the eternal, *present*.

For many years and for many people, Timberline Ranch was synonymous with Rocky. Rocky was an imperfect man with perfect vision when it came to walking toward his Lord. When I read the gospels, I cannot think of a man more aptly named after the apostle Peter, whom Jesus renamed the equivalent of 'Rocky.' Rocky was exuberant and passionate about his mission; he was able to quickly engage with diverse individuals, young and old, regardless of lifestyle, background, creed or culture. As a youngster, I admired this energetic man in the cowboy hat and likened him to a 'real' Roy Rogers; the fact that he rode Patches, a palomino like Trigger, further cemented this image in my mind!

Rocky quickly became to me the kind man that let me attend my first Timberline camp on a 'work scholarship,' because he recognized my horse-crazy desperation and our family's tight budget. It would not have been possible for me to have attended camp without this break. Through my teenage years, Rocky very much held the position of a surrogate father, as, like most adolescents, it was much easier to be authentic outside your natural family.

Rocky was an extremely busy man, but somehow he managed to let you know that he saw you as an individual and recognized your worth. Rocky looked beyond the façade of our teenage angst and rebellion and simply held to the clear, uncomplicated, dogma-free truth of God's love as demonstrated by Jesus Christ.

Throughout those teen years, I had a lot of 'issues' with the church and who was 'in' and who was 'out.' Rocky at his essence was one thing: a follower of Jesus Christ. He had a way of cutting through the theological knots and snarls that my mind created, and the fog of dogma that threatened to blind me. Through Rocky I learned that the truth is not a series of memorizeable facts; rather, truth is a Person; the Person of Jesus Christ. The Good News was, and is, that simple, that complex, and that profound.

I know that many, many campers and young staff saw Rocky in the same light of surrogate father, pastor, and mentor. After talking with others, I found that often parents had to hear a lot about Rocky, and I'm sure many dads felt twinges of that emotionally uncomfortable syndrome known as 'nose-out-of-joint' often occurring post Timberline!

Rocky and Timberline somehow invaded our brains, and we were not at all discrete about it.

When I asked one of the 'Timberline kids' who spent his summers at Timberline with his family what most stood out in his memory of TR as a kid, he answered with one word, *"Rocky."* I asked him to explain. "He was always ready to have us tag along and 'help.' He would take us along with him to go pick up supplies, or see horses. We were just kids, but we counted." He remembers feeling heartbroken that the summer was almost over and that he and his family would be leaving the ranch for home, an entire province away from Timberline. He scraped up his pennies and went to Rocky, sobbing, and tried to give him the money "so that he could stay at Timberline." This story would be tragic, if it led you to believe that he was from a terrible home! Not true! He was—and is—a very loved son of one of the Timberline pillar families—he simply was a kid suffering from a case of Rocky and Timberline-itis.

Two other Timberline kids have similar feelings about the ranch and Rocky. Levi and her sisters remember Rocky taking them and Kermit on a special outing to the Pacific National Exhibition every year after the camping season was finished. The girls would get all dressed up and Rocky would wear a suit and coat. Rocky would, as Levi recalls, "Let us go on as many fair rides as we wanted—which was so amazing to us!" Rocky would then take them all out to the White Spot for dinner before heading home to the ranch. Quite the 'grown up' outing each year for the Timberline kids!

Jinx said to me that when she was a camper, she would come home from Timberline and cry for days. "Rocky was like a second dad, and Timberline a second home to me." She would spend the winter writing letters to Timberline friends and "babysitting to make money to go back to Timberline next summer. Why wouldn't I miss Timberline?

113

Timberline was where I accepted Christ personally on the big rock behind the cabins." She added, with a laugh, in typical Jinx fashion, "Incidentally, that big rock is where I learned to whistle, too!"

I remember sitting in Candy's Cave with Nik, Odz, Jinx and others lamenting that the summer was nearly over, and Nik telling us about carving the TR brand into every desk she sat in at her school. I can just see her mooning about Timberline and Princess instead of learning French and Algebra. How do I know this? Because I was doing the same thing. I also maniacally saved Timberline brochures, letters, the Timberline Times, pictures, an expired Tuck card, a horseshoe, and virtually anything with 'Timberline Ranch' on it to hold me until the next camping season. Yes, we were 'Timberline junkies!' But it wasn't just us, somehow Timberline 'invaded' even the 'Timberline pillars.'

Curly and Curlette shared with me that during the winter, back at home after a summer of camp, their kids would often "'pretend Goose Lake' in our basement. They would start at the top of the stairs and sing, 'We are the Campers of Timberline!' and then hike down the stairs to a flashlight on the floor (their campfire)." If you think that only the kids were involved in this, think again—Curly and Curlette were right in there! I can almost smell the S'Mores in the oven!

Swede and Swedie confessed that they experienced the invasion of TR into their brains, too, after they returned from a summer at the ranch to their home in Idaho. Swedie told me, "One night there was a big storm over our house, and right in the middle of it, one of our kids came to our bedroom door, saying they were scared of the thunder and lightning. In my half sleep, I remember saying, 'Go back to your cabin,' and hearing Swede say, 'Where is your counselor?" Well, I'm not quite sure if that was truly a case of Timberline-itis, or simply of sheer exhaustion!

Upon this rock

The Timberline experience always included an inimitable combination of exhaustion and energy; humor and tears; common sense and complete, out-of-the-box-genius wackiness. Timberline was people; Timberline was Rocky; Timberline was where people heard the call of the Redeemer. There can be no greater draw than that.

In *Toby's Timberline*, I have one final memory to share.

I am sitting on the large rock behind the old horse barn. I am not alone; I am with another Timberline staff member. That week we are kitchen workers. We are watching the stars and listening from a distance to Swede's guitar as he leads the campfire. Swede is singing, with Swedie, "*Daddy Sang Bass*," and the teen campers are joining in as they become familiar with the chorus.

The staff member who I am with is restless and unhappy. She has been sent to the ranch to be 'straightened out' and removed from friends that are leading her into high risk behaviors.

Summer is nearly over. There is already a slight chill in the air, although the frogs are just as loud and the mosquitos unfazed by the cooler breeze. We sit upon the lichen rich rock; it is still holding the warmth of the sun. I am silent, but my friend is sighing and fidgety and talking about feeling 'not right.'

Another staff member joins us. "Are you two okay?" In the glow of the flashlight, he sees us nod and settles down on the rock beside us, looking at the stars, listening to Swede at campfire. I wish I were there in the familiar glow. I wish we all were, but I know that something is happening here, on the rock, now. I know as sure as the breeze that we are surrounded by angels and prayers and that the world of man and the eternal One have met for time and eternity upon that rock. It is her time.

She begins, eyes open, talking to the heavens, smiling, crying, stumbling, wanting to be called by name. Open to miracles. I laugh with her, joy living with us on that rock, on that night as we swat mosquitos and pray. Out of the corner of my eye, I catch the shimmering movement of wings touching atmosphere. A small miracle, highlighting the bigger wonder, like a comet's tail streaking after the main event.

On her face, I see the Son.

In the Garden *(by C. Austin Miles, 1912)*

I come to the garden alone
While the dew is still on the roses
And the voice I hear falling on my ear
The Son of God discloses.

And He walks with me, and He talks with me,
And He tells me I am His own;
And the joy we share as we tarry there,
None other has ever known.

He speaks, and the sound of His voice,
Is so sweet the birds hush their singing,
And the melody that He gave to me
Within my heart is ringing.

I'd stay in the garden with Him
Though the night around me be falling,
But He bids me go; through the world of woe
His voice to me is calling.

Rockette's Story
The History of Timberline Ranch

**Rocky and Rockette
(Peter and Doris Wittenberg)**

Preface

A history of Timberline Ranch, you ask? Well—yes, I suppose it is needed. So often those who begin a work, and those who follow through the hard times, are forgotten, or simply unknown to present generations. Not that we are all about that—being remembered and honoured like old war heroes or the like—but we cannot let the wonderful memories of answered prayer, the miracles that God did for us in those early years simply slip away.

Timberline Ranch as it stands today, a solid ministry beloved by literally thousands of children and young adults, now grown, now with children of their own, is the result of much answered prayer, faith in a God who loves, and back-breaking, hard work.

I am not a writer. I'm sure others could do better, but I will try and relate some memories, tracing God's leading during the early years of Timberline Ranch--from 1960 to 1983. Those early years are vivid; later, memories became submerged in the busy life we experienced in our years as Ranch Directors. Many of you reading this could write books of Timberline memories. I hope you will!

I want to give "honour to whom honour is due," as Romans 13:7 says. Many have had a part to play in the birth and growth of Timberline Ranch. Many, many people expressed interest in the work, offering encouragement when most needed. Others funded Timberline when funds were scarce! Some folks we did not know, others we have—regrettably—forgotten over the years. But to all of you, who did service "as unto the Lord," our God remembers! He will, in his great love, reward you accordingly (Matthew 10:42).

A Word about the Board of Directors ...

Timberline Ranch, being a non-profit society, has a board of directors who are chosen from interested and participating folk. The term is, generally, for three years, and then new members are voted in on a rotating basis, so that there is always a mix of new as well as experienced members. Reports are provided to the members each month, and to the public and governments, once a year.

Over the years 1967–1984 many have served and shared their talents with us. In alphabetical order they are:

Peter Allinger	Ross Gamble	John Reeves
Kjell Aalhaus	Walker Gervan	Neville Sprinks
Len Backlin	Henry Harder	Lawrence Swift
Alf Barber	Mary Harvey	Leslie Simonson
W.H. Brooks	Ron Hoskyn	Dave Standerwich
Al Best	Ted Hall	Bill Thiessen
Eric Best	Brian Kerr	Bud Uren
John Dyck	John Kinney	Kay Westcott
Arnold Essler	Jake Jantzen	Peter Wittenberg
Walter Engler	Cecil Leng	Al Williams
Gordon Fowler	Don Lawrie	Doris Wittenberg
John Garrod	Don Layland	Ken White
Claud Gelines	Jean Matheson	Jack Wittenberg
	Bob Ostrosser	

TIMBERLINE
RANCH
SUMMER
CAMPS
If the experiences
of thousands
of young folks
from the Lower
Mainland and
FUN!

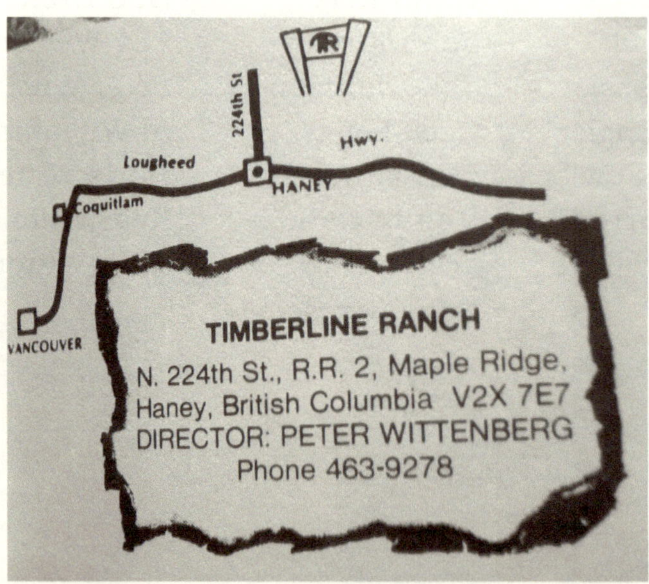

224th St
Hwy.
Lougheed
HANEY
Coquitlam
VANCOUVER
TIMBERLINE RANCH
N. 224th St., R.R. 2, Maple Ridge,
Haney, British Columbia V2X 7E7
DIRECTOR: PETER WITTENBERG
Phone 463-9278

1

Beginnings

Everything has a beginning. As a general rule, most churches, missions, camps, and even businesses are started because someone identifies a need. Then, three things happen:

> *First,* that person prays about the need and their part in it.
>
> *Second,* they share their thoughts and prayers with someone else.
>
> *Third,* if they received positive support from the person they shared with, they begin to do something about the need.

So it was with the beginnings of Timberline Ranch.

The conversation probably started like this: "You know, Joyce, I sure would love to have a farm, or someplace in the country, where I could take these school kids for the weekend. Just to get them out of the city and into a different environment for a few days." And the wheels began turning.

Joyce and Cecil Lang lived in Vancouver. Cecil (or "Cec" as he has always been called) was a school counselor. In the 1960's many of the kids he came into contact with were referred to as "juvenile delinquents." Cec saw the need of these kids, and the more he pondered that need, the more these children and adolescents burdened his heart. He began to pray about it.

Then, he began to speak about this need. Cec and Joyce were active in church fellowship at the Alliance Church on Tenth and Ontario in Vancouver. Cec shared his burden with his friends and the pastors at the church. Well, Reverend Peter and Doris Wittenberg had a three acre property in the wilds of Maple Ridge, BC, about an hour from the city.

Twice a year, the church youth and the choir would come out to the Wittenberg's for a country outing. It was at one of these outings that Cec shared his desire with them. The need he saw, the burden he felt, had become a "dream;" a dream to have such a place for his kids to experience a new environment.

It also was the dream of the church youth—they expressed their desire to be able to camp for a weekend in the country. The more this desire was talked about and prayed for, the more it seemed a possibility. And little did they know where such a dream would lead. Peter and Doris Wittenberg would even experience a change of name! Yes, we became Rocky and Rockette, and by those names we are known to thousands to this day.

We met many people during these outings on our Maple Ridge property that began to share the dream. Walter Engler, a fine young man, offered to build an iron rack over our fire pit. This project, used for many years, was the beginning of a long association with Walter. He and his talents became a big part of Timberline Ranch development.

The History of Timberline Ranch

At this time, Rocky had a tent ministry, and one of his board members, Jake Meilke, delivered a sling load of lumber on our property to build the first bunkhouse for Cec's dream. A mutual friend, Kjell Aalhus, sketched up the building plans and we were away! Of course, no thought was given to such a thing as municipal building regulations--we lived in a free country! Later, we found out there were many regulations, restrictions, and inspections necessary to build even the most humble of structures.

Cec had never stopped sharing his vision with others. Many of his friends supported him. Cec and his friend, Don Lawrie, began step three in earnest: they began seriously to appraise the situation and to act on Cec's dream. They came out to our place again and decided our three-acre property, which we had offered, simply was not big enough for a ranch-type camp. They tried to obtain a ten-acre property adjoining ours, but were told it was not for sale. Then the found a large property, known as the Ballentyne place, which they were told was to come up for sale soon.

The first time I walked onto this property to view it with Cec, Don, Gordon Fowler, and Rocky, I thought it looked hopeless. But Cec got so excited when he saw some old chicken coops; he had visions of turning them into bunkhouses for kids! I remember thinking, "He sure has more faith than I have." The property was in a secluded area and had an island surrounded by swamp land in summer, flood water in all three other seasons. "An exciting place for boys to camp," enthused Cec.

The second visit to the Ballentyne place included exploration of the swamp island. Rocky happened to be the only one wearing rubber boots, so he carried each man over the swamp to the island and back again. Rocky's standing joke began that day, "I carried Timberline on my back from the beginning!"

Mr. Ballentyne, the property owner, lived in Spain. While we were exploring his land for possible use as a ranch camp, he was seriously ill and not expected to live. The real estate agent was waiting for word of his demise; after such word came, the property would be up for sale. The word never came! Mr. Ballentyne recovered, returned to Canada, and moved back to Maple Ridge. He was to become our neighbour, and his property was to host the television series, *"Border Town."*

Next door to Ballantyne's, a family named Francis, who were raising Arabian horses, put their property up for sale. The place was equipped with two small houses, a barn, and an old slaughter house from the days when it had been a hog-raising operation. The price was right—$23,000 for 73.5 acres and the buildings, such as they were.

After much prayer, the Leng's and the Lawrie's decided to sell their Vancouver homes and pay the down payment on the property. They would start a summer camp. If all went well, they purposed to make the camp into a non-profit society for camp work in perpetuity. They named it **Timberline Ranch.** And that is, perhaps, the first thing you notice when you drive down the gravel road and onto Timberline Ranch. The trees stretching up the mountainside, emeralds against a blue sky, or the dark forest outline disappearing into a grey cloud bank on rainy, west coast evenings.

So Timberline Ranch was born. The biggest step three yet! This would be a big move for the families of Cec and Don. Joyce, and Shirley, Don's wife, would have to leave their nice city homes and come to live in somewhat substandard accommodations. The Leng's, with their two children, moved into the little house on the rock, and the Lawrie's family of three children, moved into the older house just below the rock. The children had to be transported to school, and there were no end of inconveniences associated with living in an isolated situation.

Cec continued teaching in Vancouver, commuting daily. Don's blacktop business ensured that he also have a long, daily drive to work as well. Don put his bulldozer and trucks to use on the ranch to clear mountains of blackberry bushes and to build roads.

Few know little of the work that went on during those first years. The first project was to clean out the barn, tear out the box stalls, and visualize it into the camp dining room! This long building, sided with "half rounds," resembled a log building. It had a cement floor with drains (handy for cleaning!) and the south end was first used as a tool shed, and later, made over into a cabin. The north end became the kitchen. The old feed room (off the east side) was remodelled into a lounge. A furnace room and two wash rooms were built on the west side. From the air, the building took on the form of a cross. Joyce made cute yellow and brown curtains for the windows; sun-yellow and earth-brown became the Timberline colours.

Along with the dining room and the lounge, the kitchen gradually took shape, with cupboards, a huge old logging camp stove, and, the ultimate luxury, a sink with hot water! Joyce became Timberline's first cook, and we heard no complaints from the many mouths she fed!

During this time Howard Reaney came to live with the Leng's. He lived in a cabin at the front gate, just below the rock, that became known as "Howard's Cabin," even after he had left. We lived in "Howard's Cabin" our first summer at Timberline, and Rocky later moved it to its present location opposite the Hotel, where it changed names to the "Wrangler's Cabin," and later to, "Sparky's Cabin." Howard was a sort of all-round fellow; I understand he helped put in the old oil furnace used to heat the dining room, and aided also in installing the two washrooms. Although these washrooms left much to be desired, they served for many years!

129

Before you can have a camp, you need a place for youth to sleep. So plans for cabins high up in the woods along the rock ledge were drawn. Several had to be built on high stilts, with steps going up to them. Each cabin had four bunk beds and wood-burning stoves made out of barrels. Many volunteers came to help in the building of these twelve cabins. With little money and time, they did the best they could, thus "character" was built into every one of them. Numbered One through Twelve, they spread from the west to the east of the rock ledge along the timber line. Next came outhouses and wash stations, with water being hauled up the trail morning and evening.

Campers grew to cherish these rustic buildings. Although it meant a lot of walking for counselors and camp directors, for hauling water and night patrolling of the campsite, the effort was rewarded by the campers' devotion to "their" cabins. Cabin Cleanup became an anticipated daily event for campers, not a chore, as each cabin group tried to outdo their neighbours. There was real sorrow expressed by the old guard of campers when, many years later, the cabins had to be deconstructed and moved down into the ranch complex where they are now.

The first years, 1964 to 1968, emphasized a youth training program for up to six weeks during the summer. Practical Christian living was not only taught, but demonstrated by the leaders living in such close contact with their trainees. An average of 20 to 25 youth also helped with cleaning, carrying lumber, fencing, constructing outbuildings, the many, many tasks that remained. The first Timberline Camps for youth were two weeks long and were called, "Tenderfeet," "Buckskins," and "Mustangs." Campers totalled 110 that first summer.

In 1966 to 1968, Timberline hosted a Navigator training program. These were older university students, some in graduate programs, some ex-servicemen, for six weeks of the summer. They ran their own program of studies during the mornings, and in the afternoons they worked for Timberline. Their morale was terrific! They contributed significantly to the building of Timberline in those early years: two cabins, the blockhouse, and the cementing of the hotel basement floor. Don Lawrie became involved with the Navigator program, eventually leaving Timberline to become their director in BC, and later, Canada.

By now it was evident to Cec and Don that Timberline was rapidly becoming established and should be legally organized. Summer camps were going well, and public interest was rising. Thus a constitution and by-laws were written, the first sign-ees being: Cecil Leng, Donald Lawrie, Dave Standerwick, W.M. Thiessen, and Rev. W.H. Brooks. By March, 1964, Timberline Ranch had become a registered society under the Society Act of British Columbia.

Now that Timberline Ranch was a registered non-profit society, the funds the Leng's and Lawrie's had invested into the property became a liability to the Timberline Ranch Society; in due time these funds were repaid to them. The former steering committee of seven men became Timberline's first Board of Directors: Cecil Leng, Chairman; Alf Barber, Secretary; W.M. Thiessen, Treasurer; Don Lawrie, Rev. W.H. Brooks, Rev. Gordon Fowler, and Rev. Peter Wittenberg. A camp council was also elected; they met to help chart the summer camp programs, choose speakers, and act as a reference council.

In June, 1964, Bob and Megan Ostrosser joined Cec and Joyce in the work. They began a daily radio program called *"Happy Trails,"* that promoted Timberline Ranch. They released an album of organ music; on the cover was a drawing of the future Timberline Hotel. Megan helped with office work, as well as commuting daily to her office in Vancouver.

The Ostrosser's lived in the green house on 224th street, opposite the Big Horn Ranch.

Spring and Fall "Round-Ups" were held at Timberline, as well as Christmas banquets in Vancouver. All these events stimulated considerable interest in the camp. More and more church groups were using the facilities throughout the year; it was becoming increasingly evident that more and better facilities were needed. The Hotel needed to become a reality!

Architectural plans for the western-style hotel were drawn. Cec invited the Honourable Phil Gaglardi, then Minister of Highways for the province, to speak at a ground breaking ceremony and dedication service. A good crowd turned out for the occasion, generating further interest in the ranch.

Then the basement for the hotel was dug. Of course, mountains of dirt lined this huge hole in the ground. In rainy weather ... well, you can imagine. Kids loved it—the ultimate mud slide and ooze ball playing field! The dirt—mud or dust, depending on the weather—lasted for several years. The first green grass around the hotel was so beautiful to see, and was guarded with great diligence!

During this time Rev. and Mrs. Victor Leng (Cec's brother and sister-in-law, missionaries in South America), came to stay at the ranch. Victor built a clothes cupboard in the house, and helped with the foundation of the hotel. When they left again for South America, some of their children stayed on at the ranch and became part of Cec Leng's family.

The first annual meeting of Timberline Ranch was held on January 15th, 1965. I will never forget it due to the sudden appearance of an uninvited guest. A small group of us met in the lounge (now the tuck shop). It was rather cold, and not too pleasant in those still, rather rustic surroundings. Cec was giving his report when, all of a sudden, a large rat ran across the floor to where Mrs. Brooks and I were sitting. We did the natural thing—screamed and jumped up on our chairs! Cec, very calmly, said, "Oh, don't let a little thing like that bother you, we have lots of them around." No great comfort! The room formerly was a feed room; I suppose the rats had not bothered to move when we changed it to our lounge.

My memories of some of the roundups and banquets are vivid—for a different reason! I remember one being held in what is now the tool shed. The open side of the three-sided building was draped with plastic and a big wooden stove heated the interior. Joyce brought down trays of her home baked tarts and cookies—a treat for the many friends who had braved the trip out to Timberline. Another was an elaborate spread put on by Cec's chef friend, Claude Gelinas. Claude later became a Timberline Ranch Board Member; he was instrumental in introducing the Leng's to Ted Hall, who later, with his family, became an integral part of the summer program at Timberline. Then there were the Christmas banquets held in churches in Vancouver, catered by either Joyce or Claude.

After the Ostrosser's left Timberline, Cec brought in a young couple, Pennard and Joanne Hauge, to help with ranch work. They arrived just a few months before Cec became ill. He had surgery for stomach ulcers, and was forced to choose to either carry on teaching, or continue with Timberline Ranch. With the mountains of work facing him at the ranch and his poor health, he felt it best to carry on teaching. The opportunity also came for Cec to go into the restaurant business with some friends, with Claude Gelinas as chef; this he hoped would help to support Timberline.

Pennard and Joanne Hauge put in a hard winter in 1967. I remember one of the weekend groups they hosted—mud everywhere—and they had to have the campfire in the tool shed. They took the youth over to Burke Mountain riding school to ride, but it also was full of mud! I felt so sorry for Pennard and the group and thought, "Never again—not until we have something to offer." However, the kids seemed to have fun and for $6.00 for the weekend they probably thought they had a bargain. But I sure began to wonder what we had gotten ourselves into, as we had taken over the ranch the fall of 1967.

It was now evident to the Board that summer camps alone could not support full time workers and keep up such a large property. Pennard and Joanne left the fall of 1968. The hotel building was desperately needed for adult retreats and year-round facilities. However, there was no money in place for the building of the hotel, and no plans as to how to raise a loan—or pay it back! Some suggested that the ranch be sold. Others objected, but the question remained, who would take on such a task?

Cec had spoken to Rocky about directorship earlier in the year, but he had felt very inadequate for such a task. Rocky promised to pray about it, however. At that time Rocky had engagements in South America with his evangelistic work, and, although he loved horses and children, and knew something about ranch work, he knew little about running a camp.

Many felt we were making a mistake when we decided to take over the ranch. "What's a preacher doing riding horses and spending time with kids?" was the question we heard. However, Rocky, after he returned from South America, felt led of the Lord to take on the challenge of Timberline Ranch.

That fall of 1967, as we settled onto the ranch, Rocky thought perhaps this could be a summer ministry and he could still do evangelistic work during the winter months. It soon became self-evident that Timberline was more than full-time work. Thus, Rocky came to the conclusion that

Timberline Ranch would be his mission field. That fall also, the Aarie DeVoss family moved into the house and took care of the few horses that were there. Aarie was attending Burrard Inlet Bible School during the mornings and working on a dairy farm the rest of the day.

With spring came more requests for week-ends and, of course, needing funds, we did our best to accommodate them. It meant cleaning up the cabins, carrying up clean sheets for the old mattresses (and chasing out the mice that had over-wintered there), cutting firewood for the stoves, supplying the wash stations with jugs of water, and repairing this and that. All new experiences! I now was camp cook, and this truly was a new experience. I often wonder why anyone came back!

The summer of 1968 was our first camping season. We followed the program that had previously been set up. We also had to get into the bookkeeping, printing of brochures, mailings, scheduling .... It was a challenge, and Rocky thrived on challenge! So with much prayer, faith, and hard work, we began our lives at Timberline Ranch.

We met Ted Hall that summer. Ted was an attorney for the Swedena Restaurant chain in Minneapolis, Minnesota. The year before he had come out to the Billy Graham meetings in Vancouver. A friend of his, Claude Gelinas, was also a friend of Cec Leng, and he invited Ted (known as Swede) to visit Timberline. Swede, being a western singer, was very interested in the ranch-style camping ministry. He said that he and his wife, Marg (known as Swedie), would love to help with the singing over the summer. So the following summer, the Hall family arrived.

Swede and Swedie had three children at the time (the fourth would very nearly be born on the ranch, some years later!). The Hall family, Holly, Teddy, Shery, and two nieces, Debbie and Jane, moved into the old house below the rock.

Debbie and Jane were teenagers and were of great help to the camp during the two summer months: peeling mountains of potatoes, washing dishes, and, of course, baby sitting for the Halls.

Swede and Swedie took care of all the music, and Swedie directed the girls' camps. Their help was immeasurable and their music superb. Chapel, the Friday night banquets, and, of course, campfires rang with the music of Swede and Swedie. Rocky led the early morning prayer times, spoke at the chapels for all the camps, and taught horsemanship and riding. This became his regular summer routine for many years.

After the DeVoss family, who had cared for the horses at Timberline, left, Dale Hoskyn, who was living with us at the time, and Rocky moved onto the ranch to care for the animals and property. That spring, 1970, we rented our house and moved as a family onto Timberline. It was not easy to leave our nice home, and the house at Timberline was too small for all of us, as I had my aged mother living with us. Our son, Tim, had to spend the nights with Dale Hoskyn in "Howard's Cabin," as it was still called. Anita, our daughter, stayed with us in the house. We were now settled into Timberline and the workload ahead loomed immense. But by His grace, it became the most exciting, exasperating, blessed, and exhausting seventeen years of our lives!

Around this time, Rocky accepted the position of Senior Pastor of the Capital Hill Alliance church in Burnaby, BC. This was a heavy load, but proved to be a blessing to Timberline as well, for here we met many wonderful people who shared greatly in Timberline. One such young lady, Lorraine Smith (Nik), who later married Dale Hoskyn's brother, Ron, along with Ron became active in full time service at Timberline and have been involved in the ministry of Timberline for many years.

Along with the hole in the ground that was to become the hotel, we faced two other more immediate needs: a new powerline into the ranch and a well for water. The old powerline was condemned, and the present water system came from a spring located behind Cabin One. Periodically it ran dry during summer months. A camp cannot run without power and water.

The Lord knew the need and, in spite of a strike, we got our telephone and power poles and the lines. A deep hole had to be dug on the roadway going up to the house for the main power pole. With no heavy-duty machinery available, there was only one alternative—Rocky and Dale dug it out by hand! I can still see it—Rocky holding Dale by the feet while he went head first down the hole. Dale would fill a bucket with dirt and then Rocky would haul it up. They finally got the hole dug deep enough, but how to raise the big pole into it was another problem.

Then that prayer was answered! Ed Giesbrecht, a friend of ours, called and asked if he could stay with us over night. He was moving his crane machine back to Vancouver. Just what we needed to place that power pole in the hole! He came and in short order the main power pole was in place. Thank you, Lord!

We had power, now, where was the water? Reverend Wannop, then pastor of Maple Ridge Alliance, came out with a water-witching stick to find a good source of well water on the ranch. The first drilling hit solid rock, but the second drilling hit water. That well would serve for several years.

So, with power and water assured, we turned our attention to the hotel.

2

The Timberline Hotel

That big gaping hole in the ground reminded us daily that something had to be build on it. The board approved a $300 interest-free loan concept, so Rocky designed a chart with squares each indicating $300 interest-free loans for ten years, totalling $36,000. We felt that the loan payment of $300 a month, plus the $200 mortgage payment was all the ranch could handle at the time.

The plan stipulated there would be no repayment for the first two years, allowing time for the building and generation of income. At that time the interest rate was about 6-7%. If anyone wanted interest it would be donated and an income tax receipt issued. It was an encouraging concept, but, of course, the money did not come easily.

That first winter we went out on many a rainy night to visit our friends and acquaintances and present the plan to them. It was not an easy thing to do; we had never done anything like this before. However, the plan worked, and soon the chart was filled. Some took more than one square, and others as many as ten squares. Each person was issued a promissory note with the due date noted and for ten years they were faithfully repaid. However, some just signed the cheque back over as a donation to the ranch. Of course, this was much appreciated! Others postponed payment to a later date.

The first framing of the hotel was done on a *gratis* basis by one of the then board members, Henry Harder. Henry was in the contracting business and he supplied both the lumber and the crew to frame the building. The cost of the lumber was entered on the chart as a loan, which meant he did not receive his payment, interest free, for some ten years!

Under the foremanship of Les Simonson, the building had begun. Happy day! Often on weekends a group of men from the Tenth Avenue Alliance Church in Vancouver would come out and spend the day nailing floors or whatever was needed. I would see that they had hot coffee and perhaps a roast beef dinner, and Rocky would take their children for a horseback ride. They felt this to be a good deal: work, fun, and fellowship!

Later, another group of men from the Surrey Alliance Church came out on a Saturday and put down the board walk in front of the bunkhouse. Rocky had the sand, beams, and lumber lined up for them, and in short order, the job was done.

So you see, many have had a part in Timberline Ranch. I am sure that now they see the blessed result of their effort in the lives of thousands of youth, and are glad they gave of their funds, their time, their prayers, and of themselves.

Well, the gaping hole was gone, but the hotel, framed and roofed, was still only a shell. It was now time for the finishing of the building: electrical work, plumbing, heating, drywall, insulation. The endless list of tasks seemed about as hopeless as the gaping hole had been. Prayers continued to be raised for the finishing of the hotel and, one by one, the Lord answered them as, one by one, people offered their skill and time. Even the material that was needed was an answer to prayer.

A good electrician came and did much of the work *gratis*. Walter Engler, the young man who had made the iron spit over our campfire in 1959, again shared his talent as a sheet metal worker. Walter put in hours installing the three furnaces and all the hot water heating throughout the building. A friend filled up several squares of Rocky's loan chart specifically to take care of the installation of the huge septic tank and field.

So the building was now framed, windows in and roof on, the electrical, heating and plumbing all installed. *Now for the drywall and insulation, Lord.* And yet another answer to prayer arrived.

It was spring and the road into the ranch was flooded, as usual. A man called up wanting to bring a small boys' group out for the weekend. The person who answered the phone told him that he could not come because of the flooded road. When Rocky heard about that, he immediately called back and said that he would see to it they got in—he was so anxious for any business! The group came that weekend and Rocky brought them in by canoe.

It so happened that the leader was John Reeve from Tenth Avenue Alliance. He asked Rocky if he could see the building and Rocky took him through. John asked Rocky when he intended to put on the drywall. Rocky's answer was, "We're praying about it. It will probably be when God answers our prayers."

John Reeve's response was to say that he was in the drywall business, and that if Rocky could get a truck to haul it, he would donate all the drywall needed. Rocky asked, "You mean as a donation?!" John answered, "Yes!" Maybe that wasn't a surprise answer to prayer! What do you think!

Rocky happened to have an acquaintance by the name of Jake Gerbrant who had a large, flat deck truck, and he was not slow in contacting him. Jake Gerbrant agreed to haul the 22 tons of drywall for the cost of gasoline—some $45! So the drywall arrived shortly.

John Reeve measured every room in the hotel and marked out the number of sheets needed in each. And then, another answer to prayer. John told us that we could get all the insulation for the building if we could haul it. There were bats of insulation that had been slightly torn and could not be sold.

After many, many trips into Vancouver with our car loaded to the hilt, we had the insulation needed for the entire building. After each trip we unloaded the car, packing the bats into each room, in faith believing that somehow it would be installed. By now, summer camps were in progress, leaving no time for construction.

Then in fall we received another call from John Reeve saying his crew was between jobs, "If you want, I could send them out to help finish insulating and install the drywall." Maybe they weren't a welcome crew! They were professionals and in no time had finished every room, except the kitchen and recreation room. What was left? Spackling—and that truly needed a professional's touch. So, a little later, John's crew came back out to the ranch and did the job. And all *gratis!* That canoe trip of Rocky's surely paid off!

Ever wonder who was the first to live in the hotel? Although far from finished, the hotel was about to become home for two faithful and well-loved staff members. During this time we came to know Mr. and Mrs. Rougeau (Frenchie and Cookie), who became very involved in Timberline, and were the first to move into the hotel to live.

Besides the building programs, routine ranch work and camp groups, Rocky continued to pastor Capitol Hill Alliance Church in Burnaby, (now Brentwood Park Alliance Church), and it was here that we met the Rougeau's. Mrs. Rougeau (Cookie) was very interested in cooking for the camp, and the kitchen, under her direction, was well-run and the campers and staff, well-fed. Mr. Rougeau had a steel hook for a hand and heart trouble, but in spite of these impediments, he did excellent all-round work and was a joy to have around. I always remember him so sweetly praying, "Dear Lord, make this place a paradise for children." Mr. Rougeau went to be with the Lord a few years later and I believe his prayer was answered, for Timberline has surely become a paradise for many children.

So the hotel had become a home—at least three rooms on the main floor had! The other room on the main floor was used as an office, and the upper rooms were empty, but not for long. Soon, summer staff began to use the upstairs rooms. And even the kitchen, that was not yet a kitchen, was pressed into service: the Hall family divided the empty kitchen into "rooms" with blankets for walls and they had their own private suite! Fortunately, they only needed to live in this suite for a couple of months.

Now that the hotel was a home to many, its windows desperately needed curtains. Another potentially-large expense, another matter of prayer. Again, our prayers were answered in an unexpected way. A friend, who we did not know even knew about the ranch, came out one day and simply started measuring the windows for curtain rods. Mr. Woodward happened to be in the drapery business and heard that we needed curtains. In due time all the rods were installed and new drapes hung professionally on every window. We were so thrilled!

The next big project was to get the kitchen operational. This meant the acquisition of stoves, sinks, cupboards, flooring; truly daunting a task. We purchased a second-hand stove and in transporting it to the ranch, Rocky, who was driving, had to hit the brakes suddenly. Over the stove went, off the back of the truck! Not much damage to either the truck or the stove, but rather nerve-wracking for us! Needless to say, we were happy to see it safely installed in the kitchen. The stainless steel sinks, which we also bought second-hand, arrived with less drama, but were no less welcome!

Rocky built the large, walk-in cooler, and when it came time for a door to be acquired, he heard that Mr. Christenson was going out of the meat business and went to purchase a door from him. Mr. Christenson, out of his kindness, donated the heavy and expensive door to the ranch, where, I believe, it is still in use today.

A big food mixer was donated from the Leng's restaurant, and then—what a blessing—an automatic dish washer. Bit by bit, the kitchen became operational. We could now cook and wash dishes, but cupboards and flooring would come later. Sure enough, Brian Kerr called one day and said he had a lead on some linoleum available for only a dollar a yard. Well! We bought enough to do the kitchen and all the bathroom floors. It was excellent material and lasted us many years.

So many wonderful people. Another dear couple from Capitol Hill Alliance Church come to mind when I recall how the Timberline Hotel was raised up. Mr. and Mrs. Dawson heard so much about the ranch every Sunday, and one day they asked if they could come out for a visit. We brought them to the ranch and Mr. Dawson, surveying the hotel balcony, asked what we were going to put on the railings. We showed him the plans for spindle dowelings to go all around. Of course, we recognised the expense and expertise required of finishing work such as this. Mr. Dawson was an elderly retired gentlemen and, apparently, did this kind of work in his basement. He said if the ranch could supply him with the lumber, he would turn out all the spindles for the balconies. What a tremendous offer. So, for a few dollars he got the lumber and for many weeks we would pick up a bundle of hand crafted spindles on our way home from church. Mrs. Dawson had a gift as well—that of making the most delicious pies. Likewise, we gave her some of the ingredients, and would pick up a dozen or so pies along with the spindle dowelings.

Al and Eric Best prepared, painted, and installed the spindles. What a job! Each dowel had to be individually fitted into place. Al and Eric also donated and installed the banisters for the staircases, and the hotel began to have a more finished look—on the outside.

Inside, the big beams in the main room were covered with mud and spackle from the dry walling. They were a mess! But how to get them clean? Mr. Walker Gervan looked at them and said, "I'll do that job," and he did, planing each beam by hand, slicing away the muck and grit with every shave of the blade. Dale Hoskyn joined in and helped out, and hard, backbreaking work though it was, it was finished in no time. What a difference it made to the look of the large dining and gathering room.

One of the last big projects to be done was the fireplace. Just a big hole in the floor where the fireplace was designed to go persisted while the rest of the hotel took shape around it. "How was the Lord going to answer this prayer?" we wondered. We could not anticipate the unexpected answer!

It was like this. Before we came to Timberline, Rocky had held a tent crusade in Kamloops, BC. One evening he had shown pictures of Germany, as we had been in ministry there for a number of years. A man was in the audience, and owing to political views he held at the time, he took offence at what Rocky said about Germany. Rocky, of course, knew nothing of this at the time. Several years passed and, when we were at Timberline, in the middle of building the hotel, Rocky was invited to speak at a church in Kamloops. He did, and after the service, a woman came up to Rocky and told him how her husband had reacted to being in that tent meeting, years ago.

Rocky asked if he could visit the man. Mr. Burke had changed his position in the years intervening, and the visit led to a friendship. He was a professional brick layer and invited Rocky to see his work in a house on the big Woodward ranch. What beautiful work he did! His home showed his craftsmanship. Well, he asked about Timberline and if we had plans for a fireplace. Rocky told him of the big hole in the floor, and how the dream was for an upper and lower fireplace in the hotel. Mr. Burke offered to come and build the fireplaces as a service to the Lord. However, he didn't know when he would be free to come and do this.

Perhaps a year went by, when one day a young man came and said he was to gather rock around our area for the hotel fireplace. His boss was going to come next week to start building it! The young man took one of the boys on staff and out they went gathering rocks from the upper levels highway, which was being built at the time, and along the road to Harrison Hot Springs. For several days they brought back piles of rocks. The following Monday, Mr. Burke arrived.

Mr. Burke asked us what kind of fireplace we wanted; of course, we had little idea! However, I did say, "It would be nice to have a horse shoe and maybe a TR in stone."

The next morning we came down to the hotel and there on the floor was laid out in stone a huge horse shoe and a large TR! We were rather shocked, as I had envisioned a rather small one in the mantel piece, but we were hesitant to say anything. But I wondered how on earth he would be able to use such a large design. The next time we saw the stone designs they were standing upright, one on each side of the opening, looking, if anything, even bigger!

Mr. Burke had us gather all of the old tin cans and scrap metal we could find to pack around the two chimney flues, as the weight of the stone was substantial and this lightened the load on the floor and foundation of the hotel. Gradually the fireplace took form into the beautiful work that stands in the hotel to this day. Glowing gold and red and warm earth-tone stone contrasting the cool white stone horseshoe and TR—what a wonderful contribution to the building! The two fireplaces have brought joy and hominess to the many guests and staff members at Timberline.

By now, along with the many finishing jobs that still needed doing inside the hotel, there was much upkeep and routine maintenance that any large, much-used building requires on a regular basis. At this time in Timberline's history, we had a Ladies Auxiliary that would come out once a month in the Spring and Fall to perform much needed labour. On one occasion the ladies brought their husbands and we had a giant "painting bee." But perhaps the most constant upkeep called for in the hotel was that required by the flooring.

With the exception of the kitchen and the bathrooms, the floors were all laid with a pressed hardboard, which, we found to our dismay, turned to sawdust under the delighted trampling of the feet of thousands of children. The dust went everywhere; the floors were very difficult to keep clean and literally soaked up any amount of floor wax. Something had to be done. In addition to the flooring, we needed light fixtures, fire doors, cupboards—all the "extras" that really aren't so "extra" at all when it comes down to daily living.

One day I saw an advertisement in the paper which said that the National Housing Association (NHA) had funds available for the upgrading of older homes and for non profit societies. Well! Of course, I applied, but did not hear anything further. Then, one day, several months later, a man came out to the ranch and asked to see the director and to tour the hotel.

Rocky thought it was another inspector from some government office, as we had seen so many of them during the building of the hotel, so he wasn't overly anxious to take the time to show him around, but, of course, he did. The man had a note pad, and as he went through the building, he would write down the items that were needed: "fire doors," smoke detectors," "carpet." As the list grew longer, Rocky grew more alarmed, and silently prayed as to how the provision for this list would be provided to meet the inspector's demands.

They had reached the end of the inspection of the building and Rocky heard that the work should be done and then, to his amazement, the words, "upon their inspection and approval, all would be paid for by the government under the NHA program!" Hallelujah! Hallelujah! Amen!

Thus the hotel became a reality for summer staff, school and church groups, and literally thousands of guests year round. Small improvements continued to be made, but an impossible dream had come true, thanks to answered prayer.

3

Flood Season

Every year it always struck me as amazing one morning to look out and see a lake in front of us that hadn't been there the night before. How wonderful—waterfront property! But, as well, it meant the beginning of six to eight weeks of isolation, exasperation, and, often, hilarious experiences!

The flood season generally began in June and lasted well into July. It was caused by Spring run-off. As the Fraser river rose the volume backed up into both the Pitt and Alouette rivers, flooding the low-lying areas and roads going into Timberline. These flood waters were subject to the tides and we came to know when high tide was expected and made transportation decisions accordingly.

During the first years, the Leng's and Lawrie's found it very trying to get in and out of the ranch during the flood season, so an old car frame was built high enough for the engine to be over the water. Steps were built up to the seat and it was called the "high car." This was well-used for a season or two, but eventually came to be most beloved as a wonderful play toy for the campers to climb on.

An amphi car was then purchased by the ranch and this little vehicle could be driven on land or water. It was ideal. Although made to hold four persons, many times it was hard pressed into service and quite overloaded—especially during the Navigator training program when some eight to ten fellows would hitch a ride into town to do their laundry and run personal errands.

One time a building inspector called and wanted to come out to inspect our new outhouses. We made arrangements for him to leave his car at 132nd avenue and await transportation across the flood waters. Off I went in the amphi car out to pick him up. I can still see the horrified look on his face as this big wave approached him caused by a little red car with a WOMAN driver! I assured him that he was quite safe and he found the ride most exciting.

Eventually the amphi car could not be repaired, as parts were no longer made for the obsolete vehicle, so we had to resort to using our own car and truck to drive through the water. This meant we had to have a brake and clutch job every year on both vehicles. Just one of the many prices we paid for our lovely lake-front property! I remember driving our old car through the flood and the water pouring in across my waist. I looked down and saw little minnows swimming around me--unbelievable, but true.

Over the years we became experts at driving through water. If it was too deep you took the fan belt off so the water would not splash up into the engine. If you stalled, someone quickly jumped out into the water and began pushing; by using the starter you could go quite a distance. But there were other ways we managed transportation over the flood waters.

150

The History of Timberline Ranch

One spring we had three men working under a government program at the ranch. As usual, overnight, the flood occurred, and the next morning we had a phone call from the men saying the road was impassible with their vehicle. Rocky said, "I'll come out with some horses if you're willing to ride in." They agreed and thought it would be great fun and a new experience. The water was high—up to the horses' bellies. One horse, Merry Legs, a huge bay mare, stepped off the road and went right down into the depths of a ditch. The man hung on for dear life, but his hat and lunch bucket went sailing down the road!

We did have one row boat that we used to ferry supplies of food, propane, hay and feed. Often you could drive to the bridge and honk the horn for "boat service" to the ranch. The milk man did this every morning--when he could get as far as the bridge.

The biggest concern during flood season came when the summer camping season began and campers and their families began arriving. We would have to register each camper out on the road near 136 avenue; their parents never even saw the ranch, just the sight of their child going off through the water on the back of a truck, or wading knee-deep in water down the road. Of course the kids found this all tremendously exciting, and part of the fun of camp, especially with thousands of tadpoles swimming around their every step! But for the director, staff, and, I'm sure, parents, it was most trying.

One flood season we were registering campers down the road and trucking them into the ranch, but the water was too high even for the truck to make it further than the bridge. We had an old tractor with high hind tires that pulled a built-up hay rack. This contraption was pressed into service and soon kids and their luggage were piled into the hay rack and chugging along through the water.

Halfway to the ranch one of the big tires sprang a leak and each time it went around a fountain of water sprayed out. The kids thought this was great. Finally the tire flattened totally, leaving the tractor lopsided and unable to go any farther.

No matter, the canoes came to the rescue! The campers and staff paddled to the rock in front of the "little house" and there a chain of people quickly formed from the bottom of the rock all the way to the block house, each person passing a piece of luggage to the next and on down the line until all the luggage was high and dry in the block house. So that was taken care of—but there was still the daunting task of pushing the tractor back to the ranch through the flood waters!

One Saturday afternoon we were taking a truck load of junior boy campers out through the flood down the road to their waiting parents after a week of camp. As boys will be boys, one chap was jostled off the back of the truck into the water by his chums. His suitcase fell open and he, along with all his belongings, was soaked. His parents had planned to travel further on their vacation and, needless to say, were rather unhappy about the incident. We thought we would never see that boy at camp again. However, the next summer, as I stood out on the road registering campers, I asked the next boy his name and I heard, "Barry Friesen." I looked up in disbelief--remembering that this was the boy who was pushed off the truck. Barry Friesen came every year thereafter until he was too old for camp. Then he joined the staff and was for a number of years the head wrangler and barn manager, well known to campers as "Sparky!"

In 1972 the floods came on May 13th and did not subside until July 28th. What a year that was! For a time the water measured six feet deep at the gate. It also backed up into the drainage ditch and flooded the hotel basement. The carpet in the downstairs lounge was floating, and our belongings, which were stored in one of the rooms, were soaked through. The water spouted up like a fountain through the drain pipe at the bottom of the basement stairs. We tried to plug it up with blankets anchored by rocks, but we might as well have tried to stop the Fraser River. Eventually Rocky managed to plug up the drain pipe from the other end where it emptied into the swamp, and at least the flow of water into the basement ceased.

But there was still the water in the basement to be reckoned with. There was no place for the water to go, so out came the buckets. Fill the pail, dump it out the window, over and over again, and the water level seemed to stay the same. Finally we got hold of a sump pump and after days of hard work we mopped up a dry floor. The heavy, water soaked carpet in the lounge had to be cut into pieces and dragged out to dry. Fortunately, during flood time the weather was generally warm and sunny, which did help things dry out.

That flood season the water was so deep that for many days the only way out was by a small motor boat or a canoe. One of our staff, Swedie, was expecting a baby any day. Our 95 year old mother was living with us and we couldn't imagine trying to get her out in a boat should an emergency arise. Fortunately no emergencies did occur, but Swedie did have to make two trips out to town in the boat. The Maple Ridge emergency rescue crew were aware of our situation and ready to help us if we needed assistance.

Flood season also became canoe season. In the late 1970's we were able to get some canoes and what wonderful canoeing the high water table afforded. In late summer die-hard canoeists would despair as the river left them high and dry, but during flood season, they could canoe nearly to town! School groups took advantage of the flood and would bring their own canoes by the truck load.

153

Canoeing wasn't always just fun, however. Coming home late one night Rocky and I picked up the canoe near the Big Horn Ranch and started paddling down the canal—or so we hoped. The bush grew so thick and tall and the night was so dark, we got lost. We couldn't see where we were going and it seemed as though we were paddling in circles. Finally we hit some land and found our bearings. Then, a portage over the bridge, and a final navigation through more brush and home!

The dyke at the north end of 224th street was used extensively as a route in and out of the area during flooding. Canoe to the bridge and then walk out along the dyke. But when the tide was high, the water would rush over the dyke like a waterfall. At times it became quite dangerous, especially at night.

Undermining and erosion of the dyke was also a problem caused by the floods. On one occasion Rocky took a ride out along the dyke as he had so many times before. The line of horses followed the path they knew so well when all at once one horse and rider simply dropped into a big hole in the dyke as the ground beneath them suddenly gave way. Fortunately, neither the horse nor the rider were injured, but the incident certainly caused much excitement!

So many memories. Everyone has his or her favourite story to tell of a flood experience whenever Timberline alumni gather together—I suppose a book could be written of "flood stories" alone.

4

Timberline Camp Staff

No camp can even hope to operate without dedicated, quality staff and counselors. The many, many gifted people who have volunteered their time and energy to the campers of Timberline Ranch are truly a blessed lot, and the backbone of the camping program to this day.

Leadership training and discipleship were two of the goals we held for these fine young people who volunteered as counselors, wranglers, and kitchen and other staff. The Navigators had initiated a tradition of excellent training and dedicated service. In the early 1970's we began offering a spring work and leadership training camp to prepare staff and counselors for Timberline camps and life-long service.

Along with these objectives, however, it was essential, and perhaps a given, that Timberline staff would have a memorable, fun time! Hard work and hearty laughter walked hand in hand at the ranch, and staff and counselors, returning year after year, attested to that fact.

There are so many faces and memories that stir me as I write this. Some names elude the memory, and perhaps not a few faces have slipped out of mind as well, but the wonderful spirit of comradery and love of God, the outdoors, and, most certainly, the campers, will never be forgotten. Eternal work that grows out of faith is just that—eternal! Know that your name and face is fresh upon the heart and mind of our God.

During the first years of Timberline there were three such special couples that had a big part in Timberline Ranch.

The Hall family (Swede and Swedie) were beloved by the campers of Timberline for a number of years. Their music was (and is!) superb. Swede took charge of all the campfire music as well as chapel, the banquet and other closing programs. His ability to entertain campers by ingenious inventions became legendary! Swedie directed girls' camps each summer and her warm open-heartedness endeared her to the toughest of street kids who were sent to camp through Social Services. Both Swede and Swedie became role models for many counselors and staff who grew up, summer after summer, under their discipleship.

The Hall family spent about three months of every summer living on the ranch and then travelled up from their home in Idaho a number of times during the year for weekend winter camps. Holly, Teddy, and Shery were young children when their parents first came to the ranch, and Becky was born in Maple Ridge during the flood season of 1972. As they grew, so did their roles develop at Timberline. For example, Ted became known as "Huck" to his campers, and Holly's camp name became "Levi," as both reached the age when they could become Timberline camp counselors.

The History of Timberline Ranch

Life as a "permanent" camp kid holds special memories. Some very precious and wonderful, but, as I think our own children Tim and Anita will attest to, at times it is difficult to share your parents with so many, many, "temporary siblings" as week after week of summer camp rolls along.

Dan and Winnie Williams (Curly and Curlette) and their family dedicated two or three weeks of every summer to the ministry of Timberline. Curly directed the boys' camps, while Curlette served as camp nurse, laundry lady, and lent a sympathetic ear for those who needed to unburden their day. The Williams kids (Mark, or "Planter," Philip, or "Karch," and Cindy, or "Breeze") became Timberline counselors and staff as they grew up, and, I believe, still volunteer regularly part of their summers to the ranch.

Russ (Rusty) and Sunny Gibbler also were considered by campers to be "essential" to their summer camp experience. Rusty and Sunny gave a few weeks of every summer to minister to the Timberline campers. They directed teens as well as boys and girls junior camps. Sunny and Curlette are registered nurses, so both took turns at being camp nurse and first aid person.

The Gibbler children, now grown, regularly volunteer as camp counselors. Shannon (Doodle), Tammy (Yankee), and Ray (Slider), and all the "Timberline kids" are now ministering to new generations of campers. And who better to carry on the Timberline tradition of caring?

One of the hardest positions to fill at any camp is that of head cook. No great surprise, for this position entails much hard work and pressure, and tasks seem to be never-ending. Just as you finish cleaning up after one meal, it is time to start preparation for the next! But the cook is so very important, and Timberline has been blessed with many good cooks over the years.

Along with preparing hearty meals, these cooks taught us lessons in economy, management, and the streamlining of kitchen tasks. During those early years we did all our buying personally. This meant going directly to farmers and wholesalers for chickens, eggs, bread, vegetables and fruit. We were always on the lookout for bargains! This lowered the food bill considerably, but it meant more work for the kitchen staff as there were no prepared products. Chickens had to be cut up, pastry blended, and vegetables peeled.

Cooks that come to mind as I write this are Mrs. Affleck, Marg Rougeau (Cookie), Myrtle Anderson (Tootsie), Jake, Mr. and Mrs. Swindon, Jean Demchuk, Freda Kirkby, and Rita White. Of course there were many more part time cooks that stepped in when most needed and were most appreciated.

Of course, no cook can be without kitchen staff, and to the many volunteer staff over the years who are the unsung heroes slaying stacks of syrupy dishes and mountains of unpeeled potatoes, great is your reward in heaven! At that Banquet, you will, most certainly, be served!

Maintenance staff as well are often overlooked in their essential service to any organization. Routine upkeep and cleaning are never-ending, often discouraging tasks. How many times would we enter the hotel lounge to see it freshly vacuumed, spic and span, only to have the dinner bell ring, a flood of campers descend, and just stand back and watch the dust rise and settle in seconds! Or the miles of mud during rainy weather!

A couple who immediately come to mind is Len and Dot Backlin. During 1975 - 1977, Len and Dot came out from Moose Jaw, Saskatchewan, to help in the ministry. They lived in the rooms on the main floor of the hotel and were a tremendous help and encouragement, jumping in to fill the need wherever it arose. Len did much of the outside maintenance as well as excellent carpentry work on the "rock house." Dot took care of much inside maintenance and was our camp nurse. I still remember their tireless efforts to wax those pressed wood floors that shed sawdust and soaked up floor wax like sponges. Len served as a Timberline board member as well.

Perhaps the one staff position on the ranch that did consistently evoke romantic images was that of wrangler. Nearly all campers wanted to be wranglers when the "grew up!" Just think, living on a real ranch, riding and caring for horses all day long ... Most campers, especially junior girls, were horse–crazy, and to have a job working with horses all day long was a dream come true.

Of course, the reality of the job even today is far from romantic. But back in the early years of Timberline, before the big barn, riding arena, corrals, and good fencing, wrangling was often back breaking labour in all sorts of weather, with more time being spent on the ground mending fences, hauling hay and water, and fixing gear, than on the horses' backs. Being a good wrangler at Timberline ranch carried an added criteria: you must care for kids and be able to forge relationships with them.

In the early years Timberline camps had many children sent by Social Services; inner city kids, all with varying degrees of difficulty trusting others. Often, these kids would be able to form a friendship with a horse more easily than a human being. Wranglers, being in the unique position of working with horses, were seen as "okay" by these hurt children, and would become a bridge to these precious kids, allowing other healing relationships to begin. Thank God for the wranglers! And the horses, too, of course!

One horse–crazy junior girl comes to mind as I'm writing this. Lorraine Smith Hoskyn (Nik) became such a wrangler. She also did virtually every other volunteer job on the ranch throughout her teenage years after she was too old to be a camper. Nik, like a good number of other Timberline staff members, met her husband Ron Hoskyn (Chips) through working at the ranch. Both Nik and Chips have become an integral part of Timberline history—both past and present. They are board members and Nik has served as-Ranch Director.

The Hoskyn family from the earliest days were involved with the ranch. Cec Lang was Ron's uncle, and Ron's brother Dale (Hoss), Ron (Chips), and their sister Leane (Little Hoss), were among the first campers at Timberline. All became staff members in due time and served with integrity. Campers and staff alike benefitted by—and at times were the butt of—their abiding sense of humour!

So Timberline Ranch goes on, under the caring dedication of many staff members and counselors and wranglers who follow God's leading to minister to the children and youth of today; and we know that the precious ones they minister to now may, in turn, minister to the next generation.

**"... the plan of the Lord stands forever; the design
of his heart, through all generations ..."
Psalm 33:11**

5

Timberline Cabins
and the Bunkhouse Complex

Timberline's cabins. Something magical must happen within the four walls of these humble, rather rustic, dwellings to cause campers to come to love their little homes so well. Ask any long-time camper or counselor about it and they will tell you that somehow God is so close when you drift off to sleep surrounded by friends, listening to the wind in the trees, the rain on the roof, with the sound of horses' hooves muffled by the grass they are quietly cropping, and the smell of smoke from the campfire still lingers around you.

The first twelve cabins were built away back in the trees, into the rock ledge at the north end of the property. They stretched from Cabin One in the far west, to Cabin Twelve in the east. Camp directors certainly got their exercise checking cabins every night—what a distance to walk!

These wood framed, uninsulated cabins with their stove pipe chimneys were truly rustic. Most of them were built on stilts with plank stairs going up to them. They each had four built-in bunkbeds, and a wood-burning stove took the chill off the air. In all they could house 96 campers.

Three outhouses and two washhouses accommodated other essential needs. For some unknown reason, the outhouses became a significant part of camp life, and when the new washrooms were built the old outhouses were missed by many. Timberline "outhouse stories" are myriad whenever old time staff and campers get together!

After a few years the cabins began to deteriorate and maintenance took up much of our time. Windows, floors and roofs were forever needing replacement. Bats, mice, skunks and racoons found them wonderful havens to overwinter and were often reluctant to leave in the spring time! Each cabin, every bunk, had to be checked prior to camping season, and, at the start of every week of camp, each mattress had to be covered with a clean sheet. A minimum of ninety-six sheets needed to be collected, trucked down to the hotel, washed and dried, trucked back up to the cabins and replaced every weekend. You can imagine the time consuming labour! You can't imagine—unless you were the labourer—how much mud was ground into each sheet and how difficult they were to get clean!

As Timberline grew, and as policy changes were made in health care and social services, government officials became more involved in camping facilities and mandated more stringent regulations, it seemed, with every new camping season. First, the health authorities demanded that new outhouses with cement foundations be built, adhering to new park standards. We no sooner did this when, at next inspection, new regulations required that each cabin have access to washrooms with running water within a few hundred feet.

With our cabins being spread so far apart, this was a rather impossible situation. Something had to be done or else our license would not be renewed.

The only economically-feasible solution was to move the cabins down to the existing source of running water, rather than plumb the mountain! What a challenge, and what a source of nostalgic lament for the old staff and campers who had so many wonderful memories of sleeping under the trees. I recall Fay Lapka Richardson (Toby) telling us how, during rainstorms, the ponies sheltered under their cabin (I believe Cabin 8), and she would reach through a knothole in the floor and pet Blackjack and Topsy. Now if that wasn't rustic!

The first cabin Rocky decided to move was Cabin 7, the largest one and on level ground, not stilts. We hired a bulldozer to do the actual moving, but first a cement foundation had to be poured. The site chosen was down behind the wranglers' cabin, behind the, soon to become, bunkhouse complex.

During the move, two NHA (National Housing Association) inspectors arrived to check on the hotel project and they asked to see Rocky. They saw the formidable task ahead of us and were most impressed. More importantly, they found a government program that could help with the cost of the relocation. So, according to the guidelines of that program, each cabin was dismantled, moved to behind the bunkhouse complex, and rebuilt exactly the same size as the original. But this time, of course, on cement foundations, and with electric heat. No more barrel wood stoves, a lament for many old timers, but much more safe. And, no more bats and skunks reluctant to move in the Spring, or small horses visiting under the cabin at night!

The cabins were now in reach of the existing washroom. However, it soon became apparent that the next project of necessity would be to upgrade the washroom and enlarge the original kitchen and dining room facility. Timberline was growing by leaps and bounds.

The soon-to-become bunkhouse complex originally had been home to Arabian horses prior to the purchase of the property by the Leng's and Lawrie's in 1961. We had seen it renovated into the dining room, kitchen, staff lounge, and tuck shop. Now it was to enter a third life with bunkhouses, fireplace lounge and dining area, expanded washrooms and tuck shop.

Two things stand out to me as I remember that particular building project. One was the tremendous preparation necessary for the very large septic field needed for the new washrooms. The second was the installation of the large beam needed to widen the lounge and dining area.

Rocky had procured the huge beam from a salvage company, but how was he to install it? Not being a professional carpenter, he laid awake many a night trying to figure out how he was going to fit it in place. After all the hours of preparation, I recall the beam being hoisted in place, and Rocky's great shout, "PRAISE THE LORD!" when that beam fit in place perfectly. I'm sure the neighbours heard him all the way to town!

We were able to get stainless steel sinks, cupboards, and other kitchen furnishings from the same salvage company, I believe it was Jack's Used Building Supplies in Capitol Hill, at a fraction of the cost of new materials. The bunkhouse complex was now double in size and quickly went into action, serving the many groups who wish to do their own cooking, or run their own program, but have access to the ranch facilities.

6

The House on the Rock

With the growth of Timberline—the increase of campers, additional weekend and school groups throughout the year—it became necessary to have full time help and another home on the property. This became a real need and a matter of prayer. The answer would come, as it often does, in a most unexpected manner.

The old Buckerfield's Feed and Seed building on 224th street in Maple Ridge, just opposite the post office, was being demolished. As I drove by one day I saw a huge pile of beams and lumber and thought how Timberline could make use of that material for road building and all the upkeep that a ranch generates. I told Rocky about what I had seen, and he suggested I go back and inquire if it was for sale, and for how much.

I met the contractor and he said he would sell it all for $200, but we would have to move it ourselves. That night there happened to be a Timberline Board meeting and the purchase was immediately approved—they said for $200 it was a gift. But to move such a gift was another matter!

Well, with just an old truck and brute force, Rocky and, I believe, Dale Hoskyn, moved one beam at a time, piling them up on the roadway in front of the bunkhouse. That winter we used several for road building and various other projects.

The following summer the beams were moved into the tool shed and, during one of the rodeo programs, a man walked by and seeing them said, "There's enough lumber there to build a house." "Really?" said Rocky. Well, that sounded great, and was the beginning on an answer to our prayers.

We contacted several mills to have the beams made into lumber, but they refused because of the possibility of nails in the used beams wrecking their machinery. We kept trying, however, and one day a mill in Pitt Meadows agreed to do it if we brought it in that day, as they were between jobs. No time was lost in transporting those beams, and soon we had piles of 2x6 and 2x8 planks, ready for building. So now we had the basic lumber required for framing and we had faith that God would supply the rest.

The top of the high rock offered a beautiful view of the whole ranch. We thought it was the best place to build, however not all agreed. There was no way of hauling supplies up the rock. There was the original old house, partly demolished, at the bottom of the rock, that some felt was the logical site to use. Unfortunately, that site had the access road in its front yard, and, being right in the middle of the action, certainly was not conducive to peace and quiet!

We drew up plans and presented them to the Board and they agreed that the place to build was on top of the rock. The first job for Rocky was to build steps up to the work site; the second was to have the rock blasted to allow for a part-basement. Thus it truly is the "house built upon a firm foundation." Solid granite, to be exact, and I'm sure it still will be there in the Millennium!

Several of the board members who were professional contractors came on weekends and in no time had the house framed. Windows and doors came in from various sources and it gradually took shape, although not always according to plan. I remember one day Rocky asking me if I wanted a sunken living room: "I'm hanging the floor beams and they can go up or down." "Whichever is easiest," was my reply.

We ended up with a sunken living room with a step half way around that became a great seating area for guests! It grew into a wonderful house and became home, over the years, for several camp directors and their families. Because of the volunteered labour and donated material—not to mention all the lumber from the salvaged beams—the total cost was about one third of what the building permit estimated.

7

The Timberline Horses

Timberline Ranch means horses. Horses are the initial drawing card for campers choosing to come to Timberline. And, for some campers, horses are the first entry point into establishing a trust relationship with anyone. They have been so badly hurt, or continually let down by others throughout much of their short lives that they are 'hardened' to people. Somehow, the vulnerability and kindness of these large animals can get through when we cannot. Yes, horses are wonderful, but it takes much time, funds, and work to build up a herd that can be trusted with children, never mind the facilities to care for them year round.

In the early years there was no barn at all, only a small tack and feed room and a corral. The horses, six in number by 1967, roamed at will throughout most of the land, contained only by the barbed wire fence lining the perimeter of the property, and a cattle guard that kept them off the road. They were fed outdoors in all sorts of weather; during the heavy winter frost and icicles formed on their manes and tails, clinking together like chimes when they walked or shook their heads.

The first shelter made for them was in the present-day tool shed. Rocky quickly built feed bins inside and the horses would come and go at will. During those first winters several of the horses were lent out in the winter; on the condition they be well cared for, the "foster family" could have the personal use of the horse. In some cases this worked out very well, in others we found they were mistreated, or not cared for adequately, thus the main prayer then was to be able to provide a barn for year round care of the growing Timberline herd.

Rocky and Frenchie (Mr. Rougeau), who was a former logger, went up into the trees on the back property, felled several large trees, and hauled them down the mountain side. These became the foundation posts for the first barn. Today, you can still see those original tree posts in the, now, old barn. A Canada Works Program was granted to us that winter and the remainder of the barn and hay loft were soon finished.

Over the years several additions were made to accommodate new horses, and a big shavings bin was built to hold this bedding material. Much rejoicing every step of the way! How good it is to be able to adequately provide for these hard working, four-legged staff members of Timberline whom the campers love so much.

Rocky's next big dream? An indoor riding arena where campers could ride regardless of weather. Over the years every wrangler heard about Rocky's dream, Rocky's prayer. Today, thanks to those who followed in the work of Timberline Ranch, the indoor riding arena exists. Well used, it is a beautiful facility thoroughly enjoyed by campers, staff, and, horses on those muddy, mucky, rain drenched Maple Ridge days.

"To God be the glory, great things He hath done."

Each horse that has come to the ranch has a story, and their own particular personality has uniquely contributed to Timberline's history. Timberline horse stories abound! Also, certain mysteries connected to horses are repeatedly mulled over whenever old wranglers meet: for example, "Why was it that the largest, clompiest horse (Merry Legs) was always so loved by the tiniest kid in camp?" or, "Who made Shawnee's hat, and why did she allow us to put it on her every rodeo?"

Over the years there have been a wide variety of breeds represented in the Timberline line up: Appaloosa, Pinto, Quarter horse, Arabian, Welsh, Thoroughbred, and several crossbreds, or grade horses, as well. We found, for our purpose, the grade horse was the best investment as they retain the better qualities of their mixed heritage. The most important attribute was, and is, temperament, as well as physical heartiness and good feet. Timberline horses, although cared for diligently and loved much, work hard for their living, and are under the stress of dealing with a new set of inexperienced riders every few days all summer long.

Over time, the Timberline herd has grown in a variety of ways. Several horses were donated to the ranch on the condition their child could come out and ride when the horse was not in use for camp. This worked well in supplying needed horses and, for many we found, as the child grew older their love of the horse paled in light of a new car or husband!

As well, we were fortunate to have several foals born on the property that have worked faithfully as trail horses for many years. From the original small band of six, the Timberline herd had grown to some 35–40 horses, with a couple of second generation horses still working well after twenty years.

The majority of Timberline horses would not likely go far in the show ring, however those who have worked alongside, and "up top" them consider them all to be grand champions. The ranch would simply not be the same without the colour and excitement they have provided for thousands of youth over many years.

There will always be those certain personalities that stand out in memory, however. Tim Wittenberg recalls the following horse histories ...

Tim's Round up
of Timberline Ranch Horses

Blackjack & Adarin

Blackjack, or "BJ," as he was called, was a 10 hh Welsh pony and a real little ball of fire. He began life as dark, nearly black, charcoal grey; but by the time he was six he had lightened into a true dappled light grey. This little guy could always get himself, and his half-sister Adarin, into some interesting situations.

As a young stud, in the 1960's, BJ decided that fences were suggestions rather than imperatives; he would lie down and roll under a board fence, or work his way through a wire fence as he saw fit, and he somehow communicated this gift to Adarin, who usually accompanied him on his escapades.

On one occasion, BJ got out and went for a visit to our neighbour's property about a quarter of a mile away. The neighbour had, at that time, one of their high-priced Thoroughbred racing mares out in their pasture. BJ, being oblivious to rank or station, or the fact that this lady was twice his height, did the natural thing, and in due time a lovely Welsh/Thoroughbred cross foal was born. The mare's owner, although he was well-satisfied with BJ's foal, was upset because the mare had just returned from being taken for breeding to an expensive racing stud, but she had wanted nothing to do with him!

It was fun to watch BJ control all the other horses in the herd—all much bigger than he. Whenever we brought in a new horse, BJ would pace back and forth, cutting a line between the Timberline herd and the newcomer, and not allow any of the others to cross over to examine the new horse, except, of course, Adarin. He would then go and inspect the newcomer, and when he was satisfied, only then were the others permitted to take a look.

One day BJ and Adarin got out and went flying up the road to another neighbour's property, about a mile away. BJ had caught the scent of another stud and had gone to do battle to this interloper who happened to be about twice his size. By the time my father caught up with them, BJ had inflicted about $200 damage on the bigger horse, and was himself walking away with hardly a scratch. Walking down the road that day, BJ and Adarin in tow, my father decided that, in spite of the wonderful foals BJ threw, the little Welsh stud would have to be gelded.

Very soon we had the veterinarian come out to the ranch to do this. He started by giving BJ an injection to knock him out so he wouldn't have any pain during the procedure. BJ went down, but just as the veterinarian began cutting, BJ woke up. The veterinarian gave him another injection, restarted the procedure, and again, BJ woke up. After the third injection, the veterinarian commented that he had given BJ enough sedative to keep a Clydesdale down!

However, just as the veterinarian completed the procedure, BJ woke up yet again, scrambled to his feet and began bleeding. The veterinarian did what he could, but BJ looked in a bad way and the doctor didn't appear to hold out much hope for him. We took BJ under an overhanging roof and tied him to a post, as the barn wasn't built yet and we didn't want the little guy to aggravate the bleeding any further.

Every hour we went out to check him, but, in the middle of the night, he knocked over the post and was ready to run. So we took him into a small, unfinished building and cared for him there for the next few days. Well, one morning, there was BJ, out in the field, obviously feeling fine. He'd jumped out through the small, open window some time during the night! He was a tough little character and lived a long, healthy life after this ordeal.

Adarin was BJ's half-sister and followed him everywhere. She was a little brat at times, with an incredible will, but overall a good little horse. She followed BJ in the line up for trail rides and was very particular about who could follow her and at what distance they could do this.

On one occasion Adarin decided she did not want to go out on a ride, period. The camper got her as far as the access road back to the barn, but then she just took off for home and there was nothing her rider could do to stop her. We caught her and my father had had enough. He got on her, rode her to the same spot, and she tried it again! Dad smacked her on her side, and she went on. We then put the camper back on Adarin and watched as they came up to the access road again; Adarin gave a good, long look, but she kept on going. So we won the battle that day!

Adarin, like BJ, was an escape artist, but she had perfected her own style of doing things. She would get down on her belly, put her front legs and head under the bottom wire and simply pull herself through. Then she would calmly get up and start eating. I guess, for Adarin, the grass really was greener on the other side.

Two great little horses with strong personalities. They provided thousands of kids with happy memories of Timberline Ranch.

The $50 Horse

As the ranch grew, we were always on the lookout for good horses to expand the herd at Timberline, and the two basic requirements were an even temperament and good health. We had horses given to us; some were born on the property, and others, we purchased.

On one occasion a local horse dealer brought us a mare with a six month old colt. We were interested in this big, buckskin mare, but we didn't really want the colt. The horse trader said he would throw the colt in to the deal for only $50; we couldn't turn a bargain down!

The mare turned out to be a total loss. She was a balker—would only go so far, then would stop dead and nothing short of a D-6 cat could make her move. Then, when you least expected it, she'd take off full tilt. Obviously, we got rid of her in a hurry.

We kept the colt, who was an Appaloosa cross and rather an ugly, scraggly looking little guy, with a head that always seemed too big for his body. He had a strange, stubby mane, gangly legs, and was the original ugly duckling. We named him Applejack, which seemed to suit him. In time we worked with him, trained him, and placed him in the line up. Applejack never did turn into the beautiful swan, but he did

179

turn out to be one of the most dependable and hardest work-ing horse we had. I don't recall him ever being seriously sick, and what he lacked in looks, he made up for in personality. He had a thing for wild water: that is, whenever he was rid-den through a creek or into the river for a drink, he would solemnly start to paw the water, soaking his rider and any one else within range.

In 1985 a friend and myself went out for a day ride. My own mare was getting on in age, so I borrowed Applejack from the ranch for this trail ride. On the way we joined up with several other riders and rode off toward the switch-back on Throne Hill in east Maple Ridge.

The climb up this hill is steep and long. About half way up the other riders stopped to give their horses a breather, as they were sweating and foaming up. We looked at our horses and they had hardly turned a hair. Of course, these tough Timberline horses had just completed two months of summer camp and several weeks of weekend work—about eight hours a day, six days a week of riding time they had logged—so no wonder they were in prime condition.

We continued on our ride, and the two of us must have logged about 20 miles in total by the time we got back to the ranch. Applejack had taken the day in stride, as was his style, and I wouldn't have traded him for any of the flashy looking horses that had been in the group that day.

Applejack was a quiet, hardworking, dependable mount, and even though he wasn't the best looking horse in the Timberline line up, for many campers he was their favou-rite horse. There was something very lovable about this ugly duckling who had the character of a swan.

In his mid teens Applejack began to develop some problems and, sadly, had to be put down. Possibly he had a condition called "Moon Blindness" that has been known to affect older Appaloosa's rendering them blind. Some horses adapt and carry on; others can become a danger to themselves and those around them.

But Applejack lives on in our memories. One time we had a tour group from Europe visit Timberline. Their tour guide snapped pictures of the ranch and the tourists, and they were off. Many months later, when we were in Europe, we happened upon a slide show about Canada. To our shock, and amusement, there was one picture of a horse in the slide show ... ! Yes, it was our $50 Applejack—there for all to see, he had become the Canadian equine representative for the tour group!

Good Old Shawnee

One of the good old, reliable horses we had in the early days was a 15 hh buckskin mare named Shawnee. She was a "tub" but was fun to ride, with an odd, rolling, kind-of sideways swing to her easy lope. Shawnee was tremendously patient with beginners and refused to be hurried during relay races, or anything else for that matter. Every rodeo she sported a battered, felt cowboy hat that had holes cut out for her ears to poke through.

Shawnee loved the water. On one hot summer day a group of staff went for a ride and took the horses into the river to cool them down. I was on Shawnee and when we went into the water, we went all the way in. The old girl went completely under, ears and all. Then she stuck out her nose and shot a three foot long jet of water out her nostrils!

Our Welsh stud BJ bred Shawnee in 1968. We had three different veterinarians out to check her over and got three different answers. The first said, "No, not pregnant," the second said, "Maybe," and the third said, "Definitely pregnant." Shawnee, unconcerned with it all, looked the same as she always had—round as a barrel. But in early 1969, "Surprise," was born.

We lost Shawnee in the early 1970's. She and another horse had been farmed out for the winter to a family in Pitt Meadows. Shawnee found a way out of the property and with the other horse beside her started down the highway for home. It was a dark, foggy night, and both horses, tragically, were hit by a car. We received a call from our veterinarian who recognized Shawnee; both horses were put down as they had sustained broken legs.

Shawnee was a wonderful horse and was dearly missed by campers the next summer. But, she lived on many more years at Timberline through her Surprise.

Shawnee's Surprise

Well, we now knew that Shawnee was expecting, but did not know when the blessed event would occur. Then, one day in February, we received a call to come out to the ranch, "Shawnee had her foal!"

My father and I walked out in the field to check mother and baby over, and this little grey foal, barely an hour old, gave us the once over; as my father approached him, the foal turned quick as anything, and kicked out with both hind legs, catching my father on both thighs.

Talk about a "Surprise!" He certainly lived up to his name that day. When I got closer to him, he had a change of heart and started to nibble on my jacket, and since then has always been my buddy.

At the time of this writing, Surprise was in his 20's and still going strong at the ranch, carrying on in Shawnee's tradition. He and his half sister, Miss Wonder (Topsy's filly) were the last two of the original herd of horses at Timberline Ranch.

The Original Odd Couple

Patches and Merry Legs—what a couple they made! These two were firm friends in the pasture and on the trail. Merry Legs always followed Patches, and they were horse one and two in the line up.

Patches was a 15 hh palomino with two blue wall eyes. You could never tell what he was thinking. He was a good solid, reliable horse, but had absolutely no bounce to his step and rode like a brick. The only way to ride his trot was to post—not easy in a western saddle. To the best of our knowledge, Patches had been a stud at a ranch in the interior of BC. He ran his herd in the "back forty" when he was caught, gelded, and somehow made his way to Timberline Ranch.

Merry Legs, a 16 hh Thoroughbred cross bay mare, looked like a cartoon horse, with a big head, long neck and back, high withers, skinny legs and pie-plate feet. The farrier said if her feet were one size larger he would have had to shoe her in Clydesdale shoes. She had a loving disposition, but could be a bit dim at times. On one occasion, when Merry Legs was tied in the corral, something spooked her and she pulled back and brought down three quarters of the corral fence with her. It was clear we needed to build a new corral!

As her conformation was so unique, it was difficult to find a saddle to fit her. The only one that did the job was a 100 year old army saddle. Merry Legs always attracted the smallest campers to her—many could not even reach the stirrups. She was another lesson that beauty is more than skin deep, or is it that love is blind? Perhaps both are equally true of this mare who won the hearts of so many.

As Patches and Merry Legs were, so to speak, a "set," we retired them together. They spent their last few years up the coast in peace and quiet. I believe Merry Legs saddle was "hung up" at that time as well.

Pepper

Pepper came to the ranch in the early 1970's. He was a big, powerful, 16 hh strawberry roan. He was full of energy but well-trained and a joy to ride, if you were an experienced rider. My father used him as a lead horse on trail rides because he was a quick and sensitive animal.

In 1976, during a camp, we had a near tragedy. The morning ride had gone well, and the horses were put into their stalls for the lunch break. After he ate, my father went down to the barn to prepare to take the afternoon ride out. I followed him, but he reached the barn a few minutes before me. As I entered the barn, I heard the thud of hooves and my father yelling. Dad had gone into Pepper's stall, a tie stall, to tie a jacket onto Pepper's saddle. The movement had spooked the horse.

Pepper had jumped forward, crashed into the feed bin and front of the stall, panicked, and started to kick. The first kick got my father on both thighs; as I ran around the corner, I saw him get kicked in the ribs and start to fall. At that moment, I grabbed him and pulled him out of reach; the third kick, in all likelihood, would have hit him in the head.

My father realized that this had been of his doing and did not blame or punish Pepper. He had no serious injuries, but was sore for some time. Unfortunately, Pepper was never the same after this, so we had to sell him. For such a beautiful, sensitive animal, finding a new home was for the best.

A Real Princess

Princess was aptly named: she exuded a certain quality of dignity and grace that I've never seen in another horse. She was a beautiful 15 hh pinto mare. As a result of being mistreated sometime in her early life, she was head shy and let very few people touch her ears. It took a special knack to bridle her, and while there were those who could get the job done, to Princess's satisfaction there were only three people who could bridle her properly.

While she took the bit with no trouble, you had to flip the single strap behind her ears while she dropped her head, and quickly do up the strap in one motion. It took time, patience and trust to learn this, but Princess was a horse worth the effort.

Princess was a favourite ride for the wranglers, as she had a smooth gait and her reactions were immediate, yielding to just a shift in the rider's weight. She was particular in the amount of rein she preferred; she would tuck her head and give a series of quick tugs to the reins if the rider was holding them too tight to her liking.

In the spring of 1974 we took Princess up the road to a pinto stallion for breeding. Eleven months later she delivered a beautiful, healthy little filly whom we named Princess Tara.

Tara, trained by Nik, turned into a horse worthy of her mother's legacy, and is still on the ranch to this day.
After Mount St Helen erupted many horses contracted a respiratory illness called "Leeves" as a result of the falling ash. We lost Princess, along with several other horses, to this illness.

Princess will long be remembered. She was very special to many wranglers who appreciated her uniqueness. It is unlikely a horse with her qualities will cross our path again.

Beware! Guard Horse!

Dusky was a 14 hh dun grade mare, and while she was a good mount, she was very fussy as to who was in front or behind her in the line. She would really get her nose out of joint if she got slotted in the "wrong" spot, and would whirl around, teeth bared and ears flat, at the unsuspecting horse behind her. The camper on her back, as well as the one behind her, got a real scare, as you can imagine!

She seemed to take a lot of things personally, and one in particular was that she elected herself, not only "line order keeper," but "guardian of the pasture." With each new incoming group of campers we made it very clear NOT to go into the pasture when the horses were out grazing. It's never a good idea if you don't know the horses; also this was the horses "time off," and they needed a much deserved break from people. But, our rule had more to do with one horse in particular. Our "guard horse," Dusky, could give you a good scare if you didn't know how to respond to her.

One day a boy didn't heed our warning and went into the field to pet the horses. By the time we spotted him he was halfway across the field. When we shouted out to him, he turned around. But Dusky had already spotted him. I saw trouble coming on four dun-coloured legs; this mare was flying towards him, ears flat and teeth bared. I never saw a kid run so fast, but even so, he beat her to the fence by only three short feet.

Dusky tried the same stunt on me one time, however, I knew what to do. She came charging at me, her "guard" face on and I stood my ground and yelled at her. She stopped short a few feet away from me and as I admonished her, her ears came up and her expression changed to, "Who me?!"

I loved the fussy mare, but it was clear that she wasn't cut out to be a camp horse, so we had to find her a new home.

A New Arrival

In 1975 a donkey named Josh found his way to the ranch. As they do with any new member of the herd, the horses were curious and eager to get acquainted and sort out the newcomer. They were doubly curious about Josh, who, I'm sure, sent off a decidedly different equine smell.

We put Josh into the smaller field across the access road from the big pasture that held the herd. All the horses lined up along the fence, ears forward, snorting and sniffing the air. Little Josh stood all alone on his side of the fence, peering at his new-found friends.

Unable to contain himself, Josh let out a long, exuberant, bray of greeting. The entire herd of 25 horses with one motion turned tail and fled to the other end of the field. Poor Josh stared after them, longing to join the herd, while we laughed ourselves silly!

In time Josh came to be an accepted member of the herd, and had his moment in the sun every Saturday when he became the clown in the rodeo.

Goodbye, Old Friend

On October 21, 1992, my father said goodbye to his riding partner of some 22 years, Injun Boy.

My father purchased Injun Boy in 1970. A quarter horse bred by the J-Bar Ranch in Yarrow, BC, Injun Boy was just a "long yearling," a chestnut colt with a wide blaze, with little training and no experience. My father broke him and trained him well. He worked at Timberline Ranch for twelve years, where my father and he spent many hours leading trail rides. He would also be "demonstrator horse" for Dad's horsemanship lectures, helping kids learn how to groom, tack up, and care for a horse.

Although he was a sensitive horse who could be, at times, nervous and tense, he always was calm and collected around the youngsters. He was gentle and kind and provided us with many happy memories.

When we moved to Golden Acres in 1982, Injun Boy was retired from trail riding, although occasionally he was used for short rides by my father, sister, or the grandchildren. A much quieter life than that of a camp horse!

Injun Boy was not the easiest horse to ride as he tended to cross his front legs at a trot. Eventually he began to have leg trouble, to the point where the farrier had difficulty elevating his feet to trim his hooves.

Like many other horse owners who raise and work with a specific horse, we could not bring ourselves to let him go. We truly miss Injun Boy as he was a special part of our lives.

Goodbye, old friend.

TIMBERLINE RANCH